Marjorie Camphouse is a native to California. Her maternal grandfather came to the Golden State from Minnesota to build such hotels as the first Hotel del Coronado. Her father founded the Bank of Hollywood at Hollywood and Vine during the days of Harold Lloyd and Irving Thalberg.

Marjorie Camphouse has spent many years planning classes and special programs for the University of California at Los Angeles and the University of California at Irvine.

In addition to this background, she has written academic material for the universities as well as fiction for over seventeen years.

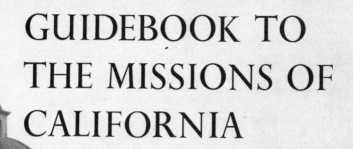

GUIDEBOOK TO THE MISSIONS OF CALIFORNIA

by Marjorie Camphouse

Photography by
Rochelle Robinson

THE WARD RITCHIE PRESS · PASADENA

ACKNOWLEDGMENTS

A very special thanks to my brother,
PAUL EDWIN CAMPHOUSE,
for his kind assistance in researching materials.

*   *   *

Appreciation also to:

Father Freelow, San Fernando Rey de España Mission
Diane Cook, Librarian, *San Luis Obispo Telegram Tribune*
Jean Rauzy, *Independent Journal,* San Rafael
The Librarian, *The Rustler,* King City
Mrs. Elsie Fried, San Gabriel Historical Society
Mrs. Margaret Olsen, Manager of the Chamber of Commerce, San
    Juan Capistrano
Mrs. Rachel Gillett, Mission San Miguel Arcángel
Mrs. Doris M. Andre, Librarian, Laguna Beach
John A. Echeveste, Staff Writer, *San Gabriel Valley Daily Tribune*
Joseph N. Portney, Encino, California
Mrs. Eloise Dunn, San Juan Capistrano Historical Society
Chief Lobo, San Juan Capistrano

*   *   *

FRONTISPIECE: *Santa Barbara Mission*

---

*The material in this book is reviewed and
updated at each printing. There are frequent
changes in mission hours.*

CONTENTS

5

The fountain at San Luis Rey de Francia.

PREFACE

In this guide to the missions of California, no attempt has been made to crown any one person, group, race of people, or nationality with a halo. At the same time, no offense is intended toward any group. Today's enlightened educators have made the world aware that greed and selfishness can exist in men and women, as well as self-sacrifice and innate kindness; also, they have shown us that honest writers do not slant material to voice their own biases or prejudices.

The student of history can admire the adroit maneuvers of a cavalry general and still not be amazed that this same man might feel larceny in his heart when he views the fertile rolling hills that belong to his neighbor. He learns that to know is neither to condone nor to condemn.

No one should—with validity—be able to point a finger at the early modes of discipline of the Franciscan Fathers. One has only to look into the rigid religious practices of the early colonists to remember that the fathers' eighteenth-century methods of punishment were in line with the thinking of those times.

Conversely, few readers, if any, of history can fail to admire the Catholic mission fathers for their apostolic zeal, and their wealth of culture and education.

The descendants of the early Spanish Californian families will certainly be relieved to know that their ancestors were as inclined to be swayed by a love of comfort and luxury as were the more aggressive settlers from the East. Paragons of virtue, even on old lithographs, are certainly cold and lacking in human qualities.

Without glamorizing embellishments, the missions of California and their gardens and grounds, stand, in this author's opinion, as the most interesting and informative historical landmarks in the entire state. *They are California!*

San Fernando Rey de España.

They are a splendid composite of art, culture, architecture, religion, crafts, and early industry. Each mission is worth not only one, but many visits to view the unique treasures they hold: the priceless paintings, carvings, and statuary; the exquisite vestments; the unique and unrivaled modes of building; the sanctuary of the gardens; and the story they tell of the early life of the California Indian.

Do not look for a plush and artificial tourist attraction. The beautiful California missions are California history in honest perspective!

Statue of St. Francis at Mission San Diego de Alcalá.

INTRODUCTION

The Mission Project

The mission project decided the destiny of the California people . . . even the color of their complexions.

For centuries the coastline lands had been the cynosure of those dynasties that speculated in trade and colonization. In the early seventeenth century, imperialistic Japan eyed the favorable prospects of New Spain, but Japan's rulers were opposed, and violently so, to the Christian religion. The Shogun had been disillusioned by the discovery of treason among the ranks of the Christian Japanese nobles. He also was disgusted with the explorer Viscaino, who unwisely reported that his master, the King of Spain, had no desire to trade with Japan.

The Shogun decided to cut Japan off from the rest of the world. He allowed no more ships to be built and, in 1640, passed an edict that "while the sun warmed the earth, let no Christian be so bold as to come to Japan or he would pay for it with his head"! Until the advent of Commodore Perry in 1853, merchantmen appeared to take the Shogun at his word.

Historical documents indicate that China made sea voyages to the new land, but that her lack of unity with her own feudal lords and princes, coupled with her political nonaggression policy, kept her from becoming a real threat to ever-eager, colonizing Spain.

France was a dangerous enemy of Spain, and a close second in her desire to spread her interests abroad . . . especially along North America's Pacific Coast. A devastating engagement in the Seven Years War, however, halted these ambitions.

The first Cossacks on the Aleutian Islands and in Alaska came to enjoy freedom from Russia's czarist rule and to deal in the fur trade. By 1812, there was a Russian settlement near

Golden Gate, and Russian boats captured sea otters along the California Coast as far south as Dana Point, just a few miles from the Mission San Juan Capistrano. Yes, Spain feared Russia with good reason.

England was mighty on the global seas in that era; and even though George III showed little inclination to settle his people on the Pacific shores (his hands were quite full with the rebelling New England colonists), dread of the English was always paramount at the missions. If there was only a suggestion that an English ship might be near the beaches, a sentinel was duly posted.

When Charles III ascended the Spanish throne in 1759, he announced that his country would rule the world. Two factions were to seesaw for supremacy in this great undertaking—the military and the religious officials.

On May 24, 1775, Father Junípero Serra received a letter from Viceroy Bucareli of Spain. Bucareli had decided to endorse the missions. The Viceroy was famed for his ambitious colonization program. Indeed his strategy might have well overshadowed that of the new city planners of today.

Time had passed since King Charles's announcement. By this time, power was fairly evenly divided between the priest and the soldier. Father Serra was delighted. The mission project was on its way.

The Early California Indians

Artifacts tell us that the Indians of Southern California had lived on the coastal lands for at least 4,000 years before the first mission was founded. In the northern part of the state, traces of Indian culture go back even further. Perhaps it would be preposterous to believe that the Indians' inherent preference for

12

a free, nature-encompassed life could be overcome in a mere forty years. Yet, this was the crux of the mass genocide of the mission Indians.

Among these natives, warfare was infrequent, and slavery was rarely practiced. Religion was regarded as a necessary evil —a thing to guard against, not to seek after. The Indians had worshipped, in a half-hearted way, a large bird which was fashioned like a kite.

Cut off by high mountain ranges from the Indian tribes of the Southwest and the Middle West, they lacked some of the more sophisticated culture, arts, crafts, and styles of government ascribed to the tribes to the East. In fact, when Father Serra first began the mission project, the Indians did not even have a chief.

Father Boscana, in his study of the Indians entitled *Chinigchinich,* wrote that the mission Indians were always inclined to pattern themselves after evil-doers. He described these neophytes as a species of monkey because of their imitating ways.

Certainly the prohibited card playing and gambling of the soldiers in the mission barracks fascinated the Indians until they were often more adept than their teachers at these pastimes. Alcohol, in any form, was as stunning as their own jimson weed, and as attractive. Perhaps the Indians liked those diversions that evoked new sensations, for they were equally fond of ringing the huge mission bells or staging a bear hunt. No doubt they had an unvoiced love for excitement which scarcely differs from that of the average American today.

The workday for the restless Indians was filled with long, arduous hours, and was well-paced by the padres, from the sunrise Angelus bell, past the noon-time meal of a *pazole* (a heavy soup of wheat, corn, peas or the like), until the Poor Souls' Bell at eight.

The padres' methods of utilizing labor—man, woman or child —might well have been the envy of modern-day operators of communes. Even the smallest of lads had responsibilities. They climbed towers to shoo the cattle or wild animals away from the newly formed adobe bricks, or to scare the scavenger birds away from the ripening fruit of the orchards by making loud beats on a sort of drum called *tule pajeros*. The men learned blacksmithing, forging, weaving, candle-making, and the herding of cattle and sheep. The women became skilled in the more delicate arts—drawn work, embroidery, lacemaking, and grinding the wrinkled-skinned olives into oil. They also became expert candy makers.

Under the *Recapitulación de Leyes*, called the Law of the Indians, Spain, with a highly ambitious mercantile program of her own, tried to prohibit merchant ships of other countries from visiting any Spanish province, including California. A few of the more daring sea captains felt that the powers of old Spain were many safe leagues away, and they proceeded to bargain with the mission fathers.

When Mexico broke with Spain, however, California, under Mexican rule, was in a serious economic plight. While Mexico did impose certain restrictions, she was extremely neglectful of her province to the north, Alta California. By necessity, the mission people—soldiers, priests and Indians alike—had to exist on the products of their own making. In fact, in 1830 the Presidente of the Missions reported that it was rare indeed to find a mission guard who still owned a uniform.

The pueblos (towns) and presidios (military outposts) also felt the strong pull for outside trade. All were delighted to find new markets for their rapidly expanding maritime services. If the Californians were actually becoming *contrabandistas*, or smugglers, the government of Mexico was found to be looking in quite the opposite direction.

Tallow and hides were much sought after by merchant ships from industrial-minded England and Peru. A small amount of trade even with the Russians at Fort Ross began, as well. The method of trade was simple. Two supercargoes, or ships' clerks, would ride ahead a week or so in advance of the ship's docking. With them they would carry a *Book of Samples*. When they arrived at the mission, a *vaquero* would ride with rare haste to the nearby ranchos announcing that a ship was about to arrive.

On the ship might be silks and shawls from Cathay to appeal to the fashion-conscious California ladies, shoes from the cobblers' benches of Boston, or casks of imported wines. While the padres, soldiers, and *rancheros* examined the ship's merchandise, the sailors loaded the holds with fruits and vegetables, or, more likely, with hides. Sometimes as many as 38,000 to 45,000 hides that had been brine-soaked and stretched to dry, were loaded on one ship.

The padres usually built their missions in *rancherias* where large numbers of Indians were living. The Franciscan Fathers recognized the Indians' astute reckoning of water supplies, game, and fish for eating. Yet, further along in their association, the padres became, for the most part, condescending to the Indians. It was the Anglo-Saxon settlers who brought the term "Digger Indian" from the Great Salt Lake Region because the red men dug for edible roots and seeds. As the University of California historian, Dr. Cook, observed, "The earlier the chronicle, the more attractive the Indian is portrayed."

In numbers, the annihilation of the Indians was great. From a population of over 30,000 in 1769, they were reduced to 1,250 by 1910!

Between 1776 and 1834, with the best of theological intentions, the Franciscan Fathers baptized 4,404 Indians and buried 3,227, at one mission alone. As the renowned anthropologist, A. L. Kroeber, noted, "It must have cost the Fathers a severe pang to realize that they were saving souls only at the inevitable cost of lives."

During the first twenty years, the Indians were lured by the novelty of the music, the pageantry and the colorful vestments. On Christmas Eve, the scene of the nativity was reenacted, and there was also the laying of the cornerstones, the blessing of the churches, and the celebration of the various feast days during the church calendar. But, as the neophytes began to die off in great numbers due to the unfortunate combination of disease and confinement, fear spread among the Indians. The fathers had to draw from an ever-widening circle of natives. That meant more severe discipline for those who were brought back from the raids on the nearby villages.

The diet, despite the growing herds and orchards, was often inadequate for the neophytes. Sanitation was pitiful, and there was only one qualified physician in all of Alta California. To add to their discomfort, the Indians were given a coarse frieze material to wear that itched them constantly.

Many of the Indians were farmed out as servants to the large land owners or to the Spanish soldiers. So, when secularization was enacted, the pattern of a type of Indian slavery had been drawn and another nucleus of hate had been formed between the Indians and the white men.

The secularization of the missions, or the taking away of the Indians and missions from the rule of the Franciscan Fathers, was not a surprise attack by the Mexican government. The padres had (to quote Jim Sleeper, Historian of Orange County) been on "borrowed time" for some years. When the mission project was initiated, the ten years allotted had seemed long enough to carry out Spain's program of colonizing Alta California, to set up garrison strongholds against the feared Apaches, and to discourage the equally eager-to-colonize country of Russia from settling along this desirable coastline.

Even so, the Franciscan Fathers might have been given an even longer extension of tenancy had not the mission lands been so enticing, with their herds of fat cattle and flocks of sheep. San Juan Capistrano horses were well-known across the nation; and the full granaries, the vineyards, and the orchards filled with fruits that were difficult to equal in size and flavor, were equally alluring.

Theoretically, the Franciscan Fathers were acting merely as trustees for the Indians, who were to be endowed with the titles to the mission lands and properties. With secularization, only the Mexican government seemed to profit. The Franciscans, with their apostolic zeal, felt that their work was unfulfilled. The Indians, who, presumably, had been taught the rudiments of self-government, showed little desire to model their lives after that of the mission environment. The all-too-necessary motivation for ownership had been lacking from the very initiation of the missions.

On July 7, 1826, Governor Echeandía pronounced the Proclamation of Emancipation, in effect freeing the Indians in an enactment which was to run amuck. (Leo Carrillo tells us, in his book, *The California I Love*, that the Governor was to suffer a more personal and major disappointment. The pint-sized, homely Echeandía was enamored with the beautiful and exquisite, black-haired, Josefa Carrillo, a cousin of Don Pío Pico; he was sorely humiliated when the sought-after señorita eloped with a much more dashing English sea captain with "violet eyes.")

To illustrate the growing hostility, Leo Friis, an Orange County historian of note, reports that Lt. Romualdo Pacheco was sent to the Mission San Juan Capistrano. The Indians listened with great interest to the fiery speech of the Lieutenant, who promised that Echeandía was their new chief and friend and would give them equal rights with the Spaniards. In fact, they were so enthused that they demanded that Father José Barona be locked in the mission's *calabozo,* or jail. It seems that the good Father escaped this indignity, but dissension was already spreading as quickly as the dreaded smallpox had spread several years before.

In 1833, when Governor Figueroa placed *alcaldes,* or overseers, in charge of the missions, the Indians found little "freedom" in supplying the Mexican government, the alcalde's huge family of children and host of relatives, the soldiers from the presidios, and sundry others, with food and products from the mission area. Thousands of the Indians, now scattered, died of the smallpox and other diseases. Some took jobs on neighboring ranches or vineyards. The Indian worker was often paid off on Saturday night with a small keg of wine. After a weekend in the pueblos, gambling, drinking, and fighting, he was ready to be auctioned off on Monday morning at the slave mart where he was sold for "only a week." An Indian could be sold for a period of a week for as long as he lived, which was usually only two or three years after he became a slave.

Land grants had been doled out by the padres at the mission to deserving Indians. That this right of disposure did not legally belong to the Franciscan Fathers was a matter of later and heated disputes between the Presidente of the Missions and the Mexican government. There were no surveyors at hand to come out to set nice tidy boundaries of metes and bounds. In fact, one Indian's property might have been situated squarely in the middle of a Spanish Californio's large land-holding.

At first, the looseness of the titles seemed to bother few, if

18

any, of the people involved. The Indians were not sophisticated enough to realize the implications, and the Californios were not noted for worrying about future difficulties. There seemed to be plenty of land for everyone; and, in the meantime, a ranch of nearby Indian *vaqueros* was "a very good thing!"

Then, in 1849, with the stampede for gold in Northern California, the entire state was overrun by prospectors and settlers from the East and the Midwest. They eyed the fertile valleys with longing, and often with greed.

Within another ten years, almost all of the Indians had lost their grants. Sometimes entire villages would be driven off by a dishonest claimant to the land. By 1860, only a few families of neophytes remained around the missions.

Father Serra

Even though they might have had cause to differ with him, laymen, church dignitaries, and government officials all acknowledged Father Junípero Serra to be a man of great stature. Physically, in flat sandals worn by the monks of the Franciscan Order, he measured only five feet, two inches.

Born November 24, 1713, in the small sandstone house of Antonio Serra and Margarita Ferrer, in the peasant town of Petra, on the island of Majorca, he was baptized on the first day of his life. The name Junípero was taken from the junipers of the nearby forests. Even as a fledgling, he was taken to the church and convent of San Bernardino in Petra, where he was taught to serve as a chorister and acolyte in the parish church.

As he grew to adulthood, Serra was elected a professor of philosophy and ordained in the Franciscan Order. Everywhere he spoke, the crowds were fascinated and moved by his words. He was eloquent.

After Columbus's second voyage to America, the Franciscans

shared in an expedition sent by Spain to Mexico. Their responsibility was to establish missions. This now became Serra's goal, and also that of Palou, his good friend. Together, they sailed on an English ship to Malaga, then to Cadiz, and finally on a ninety-nine day voyage to Vera Cruz, Mexico. The crew and the passengers were plagued with hunger, thirst, a mutiny, a leaking ship, and pumps in the hold that refused to work.

At Vera Cruz, Serra and Palou set out on foot on a trip of a hundred leagues to the capital of New Spain—a trek that took them eight and one-half months.

As excellent training for the monumental task ahead of him, Serra was given a post among the Sierra Gordas, a bold, belligerent tribe of people who terrorized the colonists. After eight years, he brought peace to the region.

Serra was now ready to begin the mission project in Alta California . . . still traveling by foot or by mule, still living the simple life as he enjoined the pagan Indians to "love God."

Speaking of his aged parents, Serra once wrote, "I wish I could make them share the joy of my heart. If they could know the joy I feel, I think they would certainly urge me always to go forward and never to turn back!" This surely was the creed Serra followed throughout his lifetime.

At Carmel, where he chose to make his home, Father Serra carried on the governing details of the mission chain and studied the principal Indian dialects.

In 1784, on a final round of adminstering the Sacrament of Confirmation, Serra traveled by ship to San Diego and then proceeded northward on foot. He was then over seventy years old, and a diseased leg caused him great pain. Returning to Carmel, he prepared to die. He had made a spiritual retreat at the Mission Santa Clara and had written farewell notes to the padres of the southern missions. He sent for his old friend Palou.

Father Junípero Serra died at Carmel in 1784. Cannons

boomed from the Monterey Presidio in homage, and for days long lines of sailors, soldiers, and neophytes formed through the grounds of the mission, many mourners begging for a scrap of the Father's clothing as a token of one they had adored and revered.

Here rested a man who had appreciated beauty; who had been enthusiastic, keen-witted, and unselfish; who could be fearless, almost quarrelsome, on occasions when the welfare of a mission—or a neophyte—was at stake; and, above all, one who had loved and trusted God with the naiveté of a child. His story is the story of the missions of California.

Mission San Diego de Alcalá.

22

I MISSION SAN DIEGO DE ALCALÁ (1769)

Mission San Diego de Alcalá (714-281-8449) is located in San Diego, five miles east of Interstate 5 off Interstate 8 in Mission Valley. The Padre Luis Jáyme Museum is in the rear of the church and tape-recorded tours of the Mission are provided in English and Spanish. The mission is open from 8:00 A.M. to 5:00 P.M. daily.

There was no fanfare! There was not even the thrill of expectancy for a long-awaited event. Only determination and religious zeal prodded Father Serra on as he gathered brushwood for the small enclosure which was to be dedicated as the first church in California. It was a mildly hot July day in 1769, and a breeze from the harbor of San Diego refreshed the workers, who were half-sick and bone-weary from their trek of two months on the rough trails of Lower California.

The mission was dedicated to St. Didacus of Alcala, and Father Serra—who always had a taste for resplendence—wore his scarlet and gold vestments. When the ceremony ended, he and the other padres donned their practical brown robes to begin the real task ahead—educating and converting the "wild Indians."

The stocky, muscular native men, with their black hair half covering their faces, saw no reason to exchange their spears for plowshares. Blacksmithing was tame compared to the excitement of venturing far out to sea on rafts and harpooning sharks that were several yards long.

The Indian women clung to their own (and, in the fathers'

opinion, very unorthodox) ways—such as dressing in short shifts from waist to knee, wailing long and loud for several days over one of their dead, and resorting to suicide when met with unrequited love.

Marriage and the family unit were strong factions of the Catholic Church. Now the padres were faced with customs that differed widely from their own teachings and caused them great concern. The Indian man usually had several wives, perhaps as many as ten. Often he would marry a set of sisters or even his wife's mother —a unique way, perhaps, of solving the mother-in-law problem, but certainly not one in agreement with the Christian marriage precepts.

Historians differ somewhat in describing the method of engagement. Some tell us that the youth would scratch the left cheek of the bride-to-be with his fingernails and she, in turn, would scratch the right side of his face. Divorce was simply accomplished by abandonment and entering into the scratching ritual with another candidate.

Slowly, despite their radical social and religious differences, the padres were winning the hearts of the "neophytes," as they called the converted Indians. Then, in 1775, an appalling event occurred which drastically set back the entire mission project. One night, hundreds of warring Indians, fiercely painted and armed with clubs and bows and arrows, crept with death-like quiet into the mission grounds. Then, just as stealthily, they set fire to every building there. As young Father Jayme came out of one of the burning doorways, the Indians dragged him to a reedy marshland and there killed him with their arrows. This was the first—but certainly not the last—real show of hostility by the Indians toward the mission project.

Despite the setback, the mission building progressed, with the church site moving to even more fertile ground. The large church was completed finally in 1813, a center of thriving fruit orchards, grain fields, and *rancherias* where the Indian *vaqueros,* or cowboys, cared for the mission cattle.

Fiestas were often held at the mission—tables spread under the trees with baked hens, beans spiced with chilis, fruit delicacies, and whole sides of beef roasted on the outdoor spits. The feasting, dancing and feats of horsemanship were always preceded by religious ceremonies, with the good fathers properly attending.

The Californio ladies, in tight silken bodices and billowing skirts, would sit atop the roof of the soldiers' barracks to watch the fights between the bull and bear or a tightly contested horse race. Indeed, these ladies were often more interested in a fantastic wager, such as two entire land holdings, than in their reputed flirtations.

These happy days were ended by secularization. Secularization brought desolation to the Mission San Diego. For fifteen years (1847 to 1862), the U.S. Cavalry was stationed at the mission. They built a second story inside the church and stabled their horses on the ground level.

By 1892, half of the church had caved in, although the dam six miles upstream, with its granite and cement twelve-foot thick walls, was still intact.

In 1915, San Diego held the World's Fair and the enterprising Mayor, Albert Mayrhofer, raised $100,000 for the beginning of careful restoration of the mission to its former beauty.

In August of 1972, as the restoration continued, Msgr. I. Brent Eagen, Chancellor of the San Diego Diocese and pastor of the parish, announced the acceleration of plans for the eventual restoration of the Mission San Diego de Alcala. These plans included the purchase of three additional and adjoining acres; an expanded museum; and special history courses to be given by the University of San Diego. (These classes have made important archeological discoveries, on the mission grounds, of more

The gardens at Mission San Diego de Alcala.

than 6,000 relics, dating back through the last two centuries.)

Msgr. Eagen told newsmen that he hoped to make the mission a cultural center of the arts with the restoration of the mission to conform with the classic period between 1813 and 1820. With amusement, he told of the difficulties in persuading the craftsmen of today to duplicate the careless workmanship of the Indian neophytes, who often failed to place roof tiles in straight lines or to erect walls that did not bulge.

The restoration is still a continuous project of deep concern to the mission fathers and to the entire city of San Diego.

Mission San Luis Rey de Francia.

2 MISSION SAN LUIS REY DE FRANCIA (1798)

Mission San Luis Rey de Francia (714-757-3651) presents a colorful religious folk play, Los Pastores, in December and an annual fiesta and barbecue in July. Every Sunday at 10:00 A.M., the well-known Padres choristers sing. There is a picnic area available and the mission is open daily from 9:00 A.M. to 4:30 P.M. It is located five miles east of Oceanside off State Highway 76.

Perhaps no other mission commands such admiration for grandeur as does San Luis Rey de Francia, named in honor of the sainted King Louis IX of France, who was canonized in 1890 for his crusades to Egypt and the Holy Land.

Father Fermín Lasuén, a stocky and vigorous priest of French heritage, founded the mission on June 13, 1789, on a bluff that overlooks the Pacific Ocean, several miles away. The first adobe church was built in 1802, with the help of the Juañeno Indians; and the present church was begun in 1811, and dedicated in 1815.

The mission was fortunate to have as one of its earliest padres the Franciscan Father Antonio Peyri, who showed a genius for architecture, building, and loving guidance of the Indians, for thirty-four years. Father Peyri was strong and darkly handsome. By day, he would labor alongside the Indians, showing them how to float logs down the river from the Palomar Mountains, twenty miles away. In the evenings, he was fond of playing whist, or arguing, in a friendly fashion, with a visiting Californio. The richness of the soil, the mild weather, Indians that were well fed

29

enough to be friendly, all combined to add to Father Peyri's successful administration.

And so, San Luis Rey became an extremely prosperous mission, suitably called "The King of the Missions" for its cattle, which grew sleek on the large land holdings; its enviable fruit gardens; and the hundreds of gallons of soap that were milled from the tallow of its animals.

As the buildings stood on high ground, Indian boys were stationed to guard the valley as well as to signal when visitors were riding up the dirt trails. Here, flags were raised to show the Indian *vaqueros* the number of sheep and cattle to be driven into the corrals or chutes. Wearing their hand-tooled leather chaps and astride some of the finest horses in the country, the *vaqueros* seemed to gain stature. They were needed at roundup time and those who spoke English acted as guides for the new settlers or Spanish priests. Even the soldiers condescended to use the Indians to track down the cattle-thieving grizzlies.

The kitchen chimneys at San Luis Rey were hung heavy with hams, tongues, and sundry other meats, which were to be smoked and then stored. Many a guest Californio was treated to the breakfast delicacy of a bullock's head roasted in the ground.

The *fandango,* or Spanish dance, has always had the connotation of gaiety—and even a flirtation, perhaps. Yet Henry Dana complained in his book, *Two Years Before the Mast,* "I found the California fandango, on the part of the women, at least a lifeless affair." But lifeless or lively, many dances were held in the mission patio for the Californios.

Perhaps no story of the effects of secularization is as touching as that of Father Peyri's parting with his Indian charges. When news came that all mission properties were to become the holdings of the Mexican government, Father Peyri felt great sorrow. He could not face his neophytes to say goodbye, but instead, late one night, he secretly left for the port of San Diego. With him he took two of the Indian boys to enroll in one of the colleges in Rome. Like most secrets of this kind, word leaked out to the neophyte village, and five hundred braves rode their horses, at breakneck speed, to plead with their beloved padre to stay. They reached the beach only to see the ship carrying Father Peyri far out at sea.

After some years had gone by, Mission San Luis Rey was to be the scene of one of the fracases of the American Army during the war with Mexico. During the first campaign to take Los Angeles, Captain Fremont, traveling up El Camino Real from San Diego to Los Angeles, came to Mission San Luis Rey and demanded possession. He discovered, however, that the mission had been sold by the Mexican government to one Juan Forster, who held it in his possession on behalf of his relatives, the Picos.

Frustrated, Fremont was very angry and swore he'd shoot Forster, who, fortunately, had returned to the nearby San Juan Capistrano Mission. Upon their arrival at San Juan Capistrano, Fremont, the scouts Kit Carson and Godey and their band of rough frontiersmen, together with a group of Shawnee Indians, surrounded the mission, determined to kill Forster. The padres of the mission were able, however, finally to convince Fremont that Forster was favorable to the United States. Fremont and his men left only partly satisfied and very disgruntled.

San Luis Rey, with its beautiful location near the orange groves and eucalyptus trees, is still spectacularly lovely. It has been used as a background for many films, but, more importantly, it houses a monastery for young priests. Altogether, the mission has a splendid quality that has not vanished through the years.

Fountain in front garden of Mission San Juan Capistrano.

3 MISSION SAN JUAN CAPISTRANO (1776)

On Interstate 5 in San Juan Capistrano, Mission San Juan (714-493-1111) is famous for its annual return on March 19 of its swallows. It is open daily from 7:00 A.M. to 5:00 P.M.

In 1775, when Father Serra was given permission by Spain to found more missions, the soldiers were rebelling. They criticized their scanty provisions harshly, and frankly preferred the rowdier life of the *presidios*. Decidedly, they did not share the good father's enthusiasm.

But Lt. Ortega placated his soldiers with the promise that they would not be called upon to make the adobe bricks—this menial work would fall to the Indians. Experience had proved that the natives did not seem to resent the task of mixing mud and straw with their bare feet and setting the molded bricks (which weighed about forty pounds each) in the sun to dry.

Father Lasuén chose a mission site a few miles inland from the present San Juan Capistrano. A cross was erected, a mass was celebrated, and, within hours, news came of the savage Indian attack at San Diego. Father Serra waited a year before he officially dedicated the mission to St. John of Capistrano, a fourteenth-century Italian theologian-lawyer and inquisitor.

The first adobe church was called Father Serra's church because the old priest was said to have preached there a good many times on his treks up and down the state. It now holds the title as the oldest church in California.

As time went on, there was need for a larger church, and, with a good deal of fanfare and expectancy, a master mason was brought from Culiacan, Mexico, to supervise the building. The

33

church, 180 feet long and 40 feet wide, was constructed of sandstone, and was designed in the form of a cross, with a vaulted ceiling surmounted by seven domes. The walls were of a prodigious width—two to seven feet in thickness. When finished, the bell towers could be seen by riders ten miles away and the bells were said to be heard at even a further distance. On top of the high tower, a gilded cock served as a weather vane, a choice ornament that appealed to the Indians.

In December, 1812, after the first morning mass, a loud roar was heard in the church. The tower was said to move, the walls swayed. Those who had come to worship rushed to the south side of the sanctuary and, hopefully, to safety. A major earthquake, however, had destroyed the great stone church and forty Indians were buried under the rubble. Since most of the dead were women, many orphans were to grow up on the mission grounds, where ten years of labor and sacrifice lay in ruins.

Then, in the late nineteenth century, national interest was drawn to the missions. Charles Lummis, in his Landmarks Club, coaxed Californians to preserve historical buildings. Helen Hunt Jackson, the small but dynamic writer of *Ramona*, so tugged at the heartstrings of Americans everywhere, in her soap-box speeches for the plight of the ill-fated Indians, that railway companies promoted special tours to the mission to see where the "Franciscan Fathers and fine old Spanish families had cared for and trained the neophytes"!

Despite the tours, the mission became a hideout for skunks, barn owls, and entire families of foxes, until the arrival, in 1910, of Father John O'Sullivan. Plagued by an incurable disease, Father O'Sullivan was dedicated to restoring the Mission San Juan Capistrano to its original beauty. He was Irish, witty, and beloved by Californios, Mexicans and Indians alike.

The mission is surrounded by old myths and legends. Probably every Californian child has heard the story of how the swallows leave the mission in the fall and return again to build their mud-filled nests against the old arches on or about March 19, the Feast Day of Saint Joseph. Many people are mystified by the phenomenon. Others of a more religious bent will claim that it is God who guides the birds. But a scientist, James H. Portnoy, whose theories have caused the brains of even test pilots and navigators to whirl, claims that the swallows use the shadows of the sun in much the same way a man uses a solar compass.

Another tale concerns treasure. Certain townspeople still believe that treasure lies buried on the mission grounds. At least three large treasures are still unaccounted for. The most talked-about one is that of the famed bandit Joaquin Murrieta, who was said to have been tied to a tree and his bags of loot buried on the spot. Murrieta's acts were so bold, so daring, that he was attended by a most remarkable band of cutthroats and thieves. One of his companions was "Three Fingered Jack," who cut off the ears of his Chinese victims, and added them to a long chain around his neck.

Legends aside, a tie with the mission's past lies in Chief Clarence H. Lobo, or Chief Thunderbird. He has been, for many years, Chief of the Juañeno tribe in San Juan Capistrano. From a small house not far from the mission, he has represented his tribe, which is comprised of fifteen Southern Californian Indian bands, including the Gabrieleños. It was the Juañeno tribe that greeted the first mission fathers. The Gabrieleños were near neighbors.

In 1952, the Indians opened a campaign for the satisfaction of ancient land claims totalling many mililons of dollars—claims which, to date, have not been settled.

"Jewel of the Mission Chain"—this glamorous term comes

Statue of Father Serra at Mission San Juan Capistrano.

up in almost every publication about the Mission San Juan Capistrano. At first it might seem to be a misnomer, if the connotation is one of a brilliant, sparkling gem. It is certainly not that. But if one pictures a piece of valuable old-world jewelry, such as a blue-red amethyst in lusterless gold filigree, then the tag is an apt one.

Mission San Gabriel Arcángel.

4 MISSION SAN GABRIEL ARCÁNGEL (1771)

Mission San Gabriel Arcángel (213-282-5191) is on Mission Drive in San Gabriel, nine miles east of Los Angeles and north of the San Bernardino Freeway. A National Monument, tours are arranged here for groups, and it is open daily (except Monday) from 9:30 A.M. to 4:15 P.M.

Mosquitoes from the nearby swamps of the San Gabriel River hummed in the humid morning air. It was September 8, 1771, and Father Serra had gathered his two cohorts, Padres Pedro Cambón and Angel de la Somera, to dedicate the site. But the murky waters overflowed their banks and took to sea many of the logs of that first building of worship, and it wasn't until November of 1775 that the present site saw the first construction of a large adobe building.

Before the advent of the missions, several native Indian families would live together in one grass hut. Afterwards, however, many adhered to the rulings of the church and their living arrangements were changed. The married neophytes built adobe houses around the mission grounds. The young boys stayed with the padres. They helped with the serving of the fathers' meals while learning the rituals and sacred music. The girls and young unmarried ladies were safely locked away in apartments called *monjerios*. The one at San Gabriel contained a pool for bathing, planted trees, and windows for light and ventilation placed high on the walls.

There was an especially rough lot of soldiers at the Mission San Gabriel. They had no rapport with the priests and less tolerance for the Indians. This military contingent seemed to derive great fun from their "game" of riding into the Indian villages, kidnapping the women, and shooting any brave who dared to interfere. The padres were deeply concerned, but their authority over the military was, as usual, limited.

Its military problems aside, this mission held a unique and strategic position—it was the first stopping place after the deserts and the fortress of mountains to the east had been crossed. Around 1826, the padres at the mission became hosts to a new breed of men. Jedediah Smith and his fellow trappers found the mission a more-than-welcome oasis of hospitality after the parching hot and wind-swept desert trails.

Besides trappers, this well-located mission had other visitors. One of the bells of the mission, a heavy bell with a crown top in the lowest row, is dated 1795. The historian Hawthorne tells us that the tone of the bell is deep and sweet. According to a favorite story a Franciscan padre, who came to San Gabriel from Mexico, recognized it as the identical one he had seen cast years ago as a young man. He recalled being so enthused at watching the great mass of melting metal that he'd thrown in all the silver in his pockets, for it was known that most fine bells contain silver or even gold to improve their tone.

During the lusty years of the nearby Presidio of the Angels, one of the largest wineries in California, with three wine presses and light stills for making brandy, was located on the mission's grounds. The gardens were extensive also. By 1834, there were 2,333 fruit trees in the nine orchards of oranges, citrons, limes, apples, pears, peaches, and figs. The heavily skinned pomegranate was a great favorite of the padres. The prickly pear, or tuna, was found to be delicious, if one knew how to peel it. Fortunately, the fathers were skilled in the science of tree-grafting.

One excellent source for this period was an old Indian woman. Señora Eulalia Perez de Guillen's age was tallied at 139 to 141 years when she died at the mission in 1878. Eulalia spoke in great praise of her treatment there, as a housekeeper after her husband had died, and with real admiration recalled Padre José María Zalvidea who was greatly attached to his mission children and even planted fruit trees in the fields far from the mission, so that the Indians not attached to the mission might have something to eat when they passed through. At eleven o'clock every day, carts of refreshment were taken to the Indians in the fields, water and, perhaps, vinegar with sugar or lemon with sugar.

The old Indian woman recalled the tragedy in 1825, when a very large and fierce grizzly bear, tied to a pole nine feet high and readied for a match with a wild bull, broke away and clawed several of the Indians to death. The Señora's journals have been translated in several accounts of the Mission San Gabriel. One, by Nellie Van de Grift Sanchez, appears in *Missions of California*.

The padres, as Señora Perez also indicated, were amusingly realistic about this new country, with its often contradictory elements. They were so realistic about this area's earthquakes that they branded their cattle with a "T" to stand for *temblores,* the Spanish word for these quakes.

Many masses have been said at the Mission San Gabriel for the victims of the 1781 Yuma Massacre. It seems that Captain Don Fernando de Rivera had recruited soldiers and families in Sonora and Sinoloa, Mexico, for the new Royal Presidio of Santa Barbara. When the party reached the two Spanish pueblos on the Colorado River, Captain Rivera dispatched the caravan to the San Gabriel Mission, staying behind with a small escort to rest his stock. Three days before the remains of the caravan reached the mission on July 14, the Yumas descended on the rearguard and slaughtered over fifty men, women, and children, including Captain Rivera and the four Franciscan padres.

As history moved past the mission, Hugo Reid was on the first organized train to California from Independence, Missouri. For what price, and in what way, he persuaded the opportunity-seeking Pio Pico to sell him the mission and grounds in 1846, is not recorded. But it is history that, after a few years, the place was unkempt and unproducing. These years aside, because of the special care lavished on this mission by the padres, it has withstood the corrosive inroads of secularization and continued its usefulness until today as a church and school.

Although President Lincoln is credited with the signing over of the mission deed to the Claretian Fathers, the actual proceedings were started by James Buchanan.

Today, the mission is open to the public six days a week. On the grounds, there are a garden, two chapels, a rectory, a curio shop, and quarters for the priests. Some distance south of the mission church, the picturesque, red-tiled house of the gardener still stands, an adobe immortalized by the painter Charles H. Owens.

Near the mission entrance is the Campo Santo where wooden and rusty wrought-iron crosses still mark the burial site of many of the padres; the graves of more than 6,000 Indians remain unmarked.

Visitors to San Gabriel Mission are treated to rare and special California art treasures. Not the least of these are old vestments of an unusual pink color which are exquisitely embroidered. There are also brass-locked books with crackling parchment, and a copper font, hammered by hand, where the first Indian child was baptized in 1771.

For over forty years the Claretian Fathers have worked, and are still working, to restore the beauty of this historical and religious landmark.

5 MISSION SAN FERNANDO REY DE ESPAÑA (1797)

Mission San Fernando Rey de España (213-361-0186) is on San Fernando Mission Boulevard between Interstate 5 and Interstate 405 in the San Fernando Valley. This National Monument is open to visitors Monday through Saturday (except Christmas) from 9:00 A.M. to 4:15 P.M. and from 10:00 A.M. to 4:15 P.M. on Saturday.

The site of the Mission San Fernando Rey de España was unique in the mission chain. Unlike the others, it was not an unclaimed piece of land, but part of the private holdings of the ranchero Don Francisco Reyes. ". . . Thus we took possession of the site by dedicating it in honor of the glorious San Fernando, King of Spain." Those were Father Lasuén's words, as he wrote of the founding of the mission on September 8, 1797.

Although we have no actual recordings of the transaction (and historians do have some conflicting stories), Don Francisco surely was sympathetic with, if not a devotee of, the mission project; for, with true Californio graciousness, he invited the padres to live at his house while the mission was being completed.

The padres' final home was evidently worth waiting for, as it was long and low, with nineteen graceful arches. Many other buildings were soon added. It is said, that during its prime, laid end-to-end the mission buildings would have measured at least a mile. It was, in fact, a small, well-administered town of its own.

The site was a happy choice and San Fernando became one of the largest and richest of all the missions. The fruit orchards in this luxuriant valley grew heavy with apricots the size of peaches, with red pomegranates, and quince. There was water in abun-

43

Mission San Fernando Rey de España.

dance flowing through the *zanzas,* or aqueducts, which were built by the neophytes to extend from a dam just north of the mission. The farmyard was filled with hogs, sheep, poultry, and pigeons. Holes were cut out of the mission doors to accommodate the hunting cats, which had been lent by the padres at the Mission San Gabriel.

The mission was famous for its production of delicate ironwork, for which the neophytes showed an amazing aptitude. In the museum today, there are locks, keys, hinges, spurs, and bells for the visitors to see which verify this fame.

Not all the stories from the missions are charming. One of the oldest inhabitants on the mission ranch was Rojerio Rocha, a blacksmith and silversmith, who had prospered on his own twelve acres until, one rainy night, when some Yankees evicted him and his sick wife. She died of exposure and Rocha held a burning hate for the white man until he died at 112 years of age.

Gold brought in more of Rocha's hated Yankees. Gold was discovered in 1842 not far from the mission, and a mine of virgin ore was reported six leagues to the north. Some of the nuggets were said to weigh from two- to three-eighths of an ounce. The sequel was the usual onslaught of fortune hunters and squatters, and, by 1847, the Americans had taken possession of the mission.

In 1851, Senator McClay and his partners purchased the northern half of the rancho; the southern portion had already been bought by Isaac Lankershim. The Landmarks Club, in 1916, decided on a massive restoration of the mission and assembled over 6,000 Californians to celebrate the founding. As each one contributed a dollar for a candle, a sizable sum was raised to begin the project while the unusual procession of flickering lights wove through the mission grounds.

Only by a happy twist of fate does one picture from the mission days remain in what is now called the Governor's Room. It is told that one day after secularization, a lady Californio was riding past the mission which had been abandoned. The painting, she felt, was desecrated, as it was being used as a roadside sign advertising "Hay for Sale." Not only did the señora rescue the painting, but she returned it when the church was being restored.

Indian designs have been retained in restoring the mission wherever possible. There is a wealth of fine architectural detail —massive hand-hewn doors, for example, with locks forged at the mission's own smithy shop, and ornamented with a snake-like "river-of-life" pattern. The Convento is long and impressive, with its extended vista of Roman arches, quaint grills, windows, huge chimney, and a most charming interior.

The loveliest of buildings built today play upon the magical use of water in decor. But the concept is certainly not a new one. At all the missions, *laveterias* and fountains were planned, but none was more exquisite than the one at San Fernando. It is star-shaped with painted decorations, and it stands in the plaza across the street from the mission.

The earthquake of 1971 caused sufficient damage to the structure of the mission church to warrant rebuilding, in 1973, to specifications as nearly coincident with the original as possible.

Around the Mission San Fernando is an atmosphere which brings beauty and enjoyment to the beholder. All restoration programs are planned to disturb the visitors, who come from all over the nation to see this place of pilgrimage, as little as possible.

Formal garden and Mission San Buenaventura.

6 MISSION SAN BUENAVENTURA (1782)

Mission San Buenaventura (805-643-4318) is in the city of Ventura, just east of U.S. Highway 101. It is open daily from 7:00 A.M. to 7:30 P.M. and taped tours are available.

The cavalcade, which arrived in 1782 at the beach at San Buenaventura, was indeed a small motley group: Governor Felipe de Neve, in full and splendid uniform; a few muleskinners; eight Spanish soldiers and their trail-wearied families; and, finally, the governor's own personal guard of ten Monterey troops. The travelers had come upon three ruined native towns where Carpinteria now stands. They surmised that the villagers had mutually exterminated themselves—perhaps over the theft of some salt, or a cache of acorns or pine nuts—since the newcomers had learned that it took only a small incident among the Indians to bring about homicide.

The location had two names. Cabrillo, evidently impressed with the finesse with which the native Chumash guided the large pineboard fishing boats, which could carry as many as twelve men far out to sea through the broiling surf, called the place El Pueblo de los Canoas, or the Town of the Canoes. But, when Father Serra named the Mission San Buenaventura on Easter Sunday 1782, it was in honor of John Fidanza, later called St. Buenaventura.

This mission, in contrast with some of the northern ones, was at first a place of content. Although the initial buildings were destroyed by fire, the navigator George Vancouver wrote that the present stone church was begun in a "very superior style."

He was equally surprised to observe the wonderful gardens of exotic fruits—items prized by the whaling ship captains—for, once again, the mission fathers had engineered a workable irrigation system.

This history of San Buenaventura was not all beauty and plenty. One night, a rider on horseback came with the news that Bouchard, the French pirate, was on his way. Hurriedly, the padres folded and packed their beautiful vestments. They dug holes in the ground to bury the statues. Noiselessly, the Indians went from the granary to the warehouse to pack baskets and strap them onto the mules. Bouchard had sailed from Hawaii, or the Sandwich Islands as they were known then. After pillaging at Monterey, he left for San Diego, en route burning the Ortega Ranch at Refugio. Then he headed for Ventura, as Father Senan and his neophytes were riding for the mountain passes, where "the snowfall came to the very doors of their huts." But Bouchard evidently had "larger fish to fry," and he did not attack San Buenaventura. Within a month, the fathers were back, beginning again the lessons in music and the crafts.

From 1806 to 1823, Father José Senan was in charge of the mission. His method of initiating changes, so different from the more robust of his brother priests, was to write numerous and cajoling letters to those who had the power—or the means—to comply. He asked for snuff and silk handkerchiefs, Catalan pens, and boxes of sealing wax. But these were merely trifles. Father Senan implored his superior, Father Tomás of Mexico City, for pictures "for the purpose of stimulating devotion among the converts." Padre Senan was practical and reasonable, he did not expect "works of art," but he did trust that they would be "neither crude nor ridiculous." And so, years later, the Mission San Buenaventura received the famous fourteen Stations of the Cross.

No sooner had the mission fathers recovered from the trauma

brought on by Bouchard than there came a scarcity of otter skins. The sale of skins kept the mission coffers at least partially full. Since 1808, the padres had shipped chests of otter pelts—each chest holding some forty-odd skins—to one Don Estéban Escalante. Escalante sold them, in turn, in the Philippine Islands, and the mission received about seven pesos a pelt. Between the fondness of the Mexican military for the pelts and the fur-trading Russians who invaded the Santa Barbara coastline, the otters soon became a lost cause for the mission.

The pelts were the beginning of bad luck for the mission. On one December morning, in 1812, a tidal wave of gigantic proportions brought the ocean almost to the front door of the church. At the same time, an earthquake shattered the *fachada* and the *companario,* as well as other buildings surrounding the quadrangle. The neophytes were badly frightened. In their hearts they were convinced that the rest of the mission would slip into the sea. Many fled, and for a year the padres kept open only a temporary chapel up in the hills. Finally, fear subsided and the Indians returned, a few families at a time, ready to work on the new mission buildings.

The 1825 inventory at the mission included 37,000 steers, 30,000 sheep, 600 horses, 200 yokes of oxen, 500 mules, and 200 goats. Steers were worth five dollars a head, horses, a dollar, and sheep, two dollars, at the marketplace. It is interesting to note that sheep were then twice as valuable as horses. In 1828, however, a drought from Monterey to San Diego lasted for twenty-two months. The wild horses were driven off the cliffs to save the grass for the steers. The animals which did survive brought only a pittance when sold.

In 1846, General Fremont arrived at the mission. Evidently he felt that to gain the buildings and luxuriant gardens would be a nice "plum" for his country. Don José de Arnaz was then the majordomo and Fremont, in order to carry out this ambitious plan, arrested Arnaz "to gain needed information." Arnaz remained obdurate, however, claiming he did not know any secret information, and Fremont was forced to release the man—and the mission.

After another earthquake in 1857 caved in the roof of the church, Father Cyrian Rubio, who believed in modernity with a passion, installed a false ceiling of railroad siding and covered the tile floor with the same "sensible" material. The rose-patterned fresco paintings on the church walls, renditions by the neophytes, were plastered over.

By the best of good fortune, the Stations of the Cross had been carefully tucked away at the Mission Santa Barbara. Yet, it was not until 1966, when Father O'Reilly saw the work of the famous artist-restorer, Franz O. Trevors, in the local post office, that the hope of restoring the paintings finally seemed possible. Trevors was engaged. He found the paintings encrusted with mildew and other growths; number eight was torn, we are told, by falling on an unfortunate member of the parish. The framer, Louis Urban, has sized, sealed, gilded, and varnished the age-old frames and added the unique touch of a border of red velvet. These pictures alone are worth a visit to the Mission San Buenaventura.

Mission Santa Barbara.

7 MISSION SANTA BARBARA (1776)

Mission Santa Barbara (805-966-3153) is at the end of Laguna Street in Santa Barbara. In August, the Mission opens the famous four-day annual "Old Spanish Days" in Santa Barbara. It is open from 9:00 A.M. to 5:00 P.M. Monday through Saturday and from 1:00 P.M. to 5:00 P.M. on Sundays.

Mission Santa Barbara, which became active in 1786, has always been one of more prestigious missions and the reasons are legion. Few locations, if any, were more beautiful to the eye. Nowhere was there a more temperate, balmy climate. Water was in good supply, as well as stone and timber for building. Happily, the Indians were intelligent and friendly. Without delay they began helping with the building of the chapel, the servants' quarters, and a girls' dormitory.

The historian Alfred Robinson tells us of his visit to the mission, where he looked upon "a gorgeous display of banners, painting images, crucifixes of gold and silver. The musicians attached to the choir were practising, and played some very fine airs, rather unsuitable, however, to the place. It was not unusual there and at the churches of other missions, to hear during the mass the lively dance tunes."

Then Robinson tells us, in quite an opposite vein, "Another door of the church opened upon the cemetery where were buried the deceased Christians of the mission and presidio, surrounded by a thick wall, and having in one corner the charnel house, crowded with a ghastly array of skulls and bones."

Father Maynard Geiger, O.F.M., Ph.D., in his book, *The*

Indians of Mission Santa Barbara, writes of the liberal leaves given to the mission Indians to visit their relatives. Every Sunday, after mass, the names of the privileged were read aloud. But when the *islay,* or *tayiyas,* a sort of wild cherry, ripened in the mountains, in September of each year, most of the neophytes made for the hills whether their names were called or not.

Conversions were many, and a second and, finally, a third church was needed to take care of the rapidly growing spiritual flock. This third church had been built but nineteen years when the earth seemed to open up. The quake not only destroyed the church, but great cracks opened up in the mountains behind the mission and the ocean waves grew huge and threatening.

The fathers were indomitable. This time, on the very same site, they built the great church of sandstone which stands there today. It is so sturdy that some authorities have claimed it to be the most solid building of its kind in California. Padre Ripoll might have been an advocate of the "do-it-yourself" school of literature, for he took a Spanish translation of a book on architecture, published in 27 B.C. and written by Polion, a Roman architect, and with it designed the *fachada* as well as the interior decorations. The good padre had a practical as well as an aesthetic mind, and he engineered 252 adobe houses as well.

One more meritorious act was Padre Ripoll's outwitting of the pirate, Bouchard. The father had drilled his neophyte charges as soldiers; and when word came that the privateer's ship had anchored in the Bay, he marched the Indians round and round the mission. Bouchard, evidently fearing numbers he could not conquer, raised the white flag of surrender and only came ashore to exchange prisoners.

Two trees often pointed out to visitors are called the Cota Sycamores. The story is that two young Mexican sisters named Cota had a favorite spot for their laundry scrubbing. But Father

Joseph O'Keefe hated to see these young maidens toiling in the hot sun and he built them a rude *ramada*. The four posts which held up the roof were green sycamore saplings from Mission Canyon. The trees increased in size, perhaps in part because of the diligent labors of the Cota sisters and subsequent waterings. The sycamores are still prominent in paintings and photographs, and are used as a point of reference in dating certain mission pictures.

Another tale from this mission involves the bandit Murrieta. The event which took place in 1853 near the mission, involves a famous *fandango* given under El Parra Grande, the Big Grapevine. After causing señoritas to swoon and their escorts' hearts to pound with fury, Murrieta, in escaping the sheriff, is supposed to have broken off a twig of the Big Grapevine and stuck it into the ground of a ravine where a grapevine more than a mile in length now grows.

More recently, in the early 1950s, the fathers of the mission noticed that the bells showed cracks—some large, some small. In 1953, the late Rev. Thaddeus Kreye, O.F.M., contracted with a firm in Holland by the name of Petit and Fritsen, Ltd., restorers of bells since 1660. The mission bells were returned in exactly the same size and shape, although their interior walls were strengthened in tone; and just in time to rededicate the mission facade and towers on December 4, 1953, the Feast Day of St. Barbara.

Today, the Mission Santa Barbara, where the altar light has been kept burning for over a hundred years, is owned and operated by the Catholic Church. It is the home of Father Geiger's renowned library. It is a very lovely landmark, graced by treasured pieces of art, Indian artifacts, and serene gardens.

55

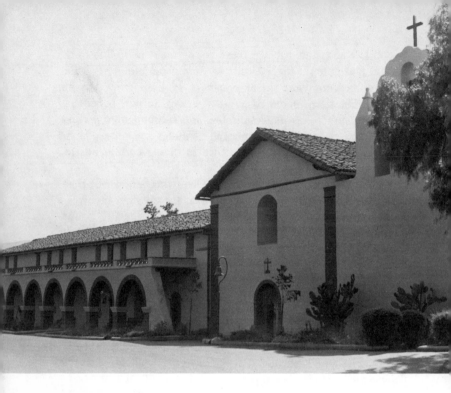

Mission Santa Inés.

8 MISSION SANTA INÉS (1804)

Located in the town of Solvang on State Highway 246, Mission Santa Inés (805-688-4815) stages a fiesta annually around the 19th of August. It has recorded tours and is open from 9:00 A.M. to 5:00 P.M. from Monday through Saturday, and from 12:00 P.M. to 5:00 P.M. Sunday.

Santa Inés was one of the three missions which were named in honor of a sainted woman. This mission, which stands on a hill near the Danish colony of Solvang, was named by the early fathers in honor of Saint Agnes, who suffered martyrdom at thirteen years of age, during the reign of Emperor Diocletian.

It was a warm September, in the year 1804, when Father Estéván Tápis, Presidente of the Missions, dedicated the site and left Father Calzada, who had many years of mission work to his credit, in charge of building the mission church. The intention was to build it much along the same architectural lines as those of the Mission San Gabriel.

The historian Alfred Robinson, however, was impressed by the fact that the building was similar to the mission at Santa Barbara. "In the front," he wrote, "was a large brick enclosure where the females bathed and washed; to the right the gardens, filled with choice fruit trees, and on the left a few clusters of Indian huts and tiled houses."

In each of the larger native villages of the Chumash Indians (those tribes in the area around Santa Barbara and Santa Inés), there was a *temescal* or "house of the sweat bath." Indeed it was even more popular than the sauna or steam bath of today, but it was limited to male Indians only. It was built partly under-

57

ground, with a door and opening at the top. The men would climb down ladders to a fire pit; then, after sitting until they were sweating profusely, they would run out to swim in the cold waters of a nearby pool, a lake, or the ocean.

Father Maynard Geiger of the Mission Santa Barbara tells us of some of the early customs of the natives—ones that would certainly give pause to the advertisers of men's cosmetics today. For example, some of the men shaved their beards with tweezers, or clam or oyster shells and carried a small sweat stick or bone in their hair to remove perspiration.

When the Franciscan Fathers brought their own methods of sanitation to the neophytes, they found the Indians clinging tenaciously to the *temescal*; although they were willing to part with some of their other, less-desired, practices.

The Indians did learn trades at Santa Inés. A carpenter, who was brought in from Mexico, was expected to teach his trade to twelve Indians within four years. Because of this training, the building at Santa Inés went steadily on until, in 1812, the severe earthquake of that year shattered the yet incomplete adobe church, as well as some of the other mission buildings.

For five years the neophytes labored on the long structure, which was later used as a granary after the permanent church was dedicated. The original plans were ambitious with sixteen rooms projected to span the front of the quadrangle.

Santa Inés had its own *estancia* for horses—for the mares and colts. The adobe quarters nearby housed the foreman and the colorful and skilled Indian *vaqueros*. Horses were never used for work in the fields, nor for hauling. Such labor was performed by the oxen. The mules were pack animals; the mares were never ridden.

In 1816, despite a population of 786 Indian converts, and

the fact that the cattle herds and sheep flocks were increasing yearly, the numbers at the mission began to decrease slowly. One principal reason was the revolt of 1824.

Resentment and hatred had been sown early in the relations between the Indians and the soldiers sent by Spain. The military, we are told, had the backing of the Governor, and they badgered and demeaned the neophytes, despite the intervention of the padres. The Indians seethed with anger until, on February 21, 1824, armed for revolt, they attacked the guard and set fire to the mission buildings. But the neophytes had worked hard on these same buildings, and, before the fire could annihilate the church totally, they halted their attack to put out the flames.

Restoration was never really abandoned in the true sense at Santa Inés. It began in 1882, a very early year, and then was resumed intermittently until the present time.

Today, visitors will not see a vastly impressive mission, but one that is serene, quiet, and carefully tended. The museum, however, contains a priceless collection of early vestments worn by the priests—some from Mexico, others from France, and even one from Spain made of purple damask with silver fringe and said to be three to four centuries old.

The altar relics are of brass, gold, and silver. There is a fine collection of missals inscribed in Latin, and handmade music books of parchment. Indian craftsmen hammered by hand the original baptismal font, which is still being used. There are also many examples of metal work which was the forté of the neophytes at Santa Inés.

Mission La Purísima Concepción.

9 MISSION LA PURÍSIMA CONCEPCIÓN (1787)

Mission La Purísima Concepción (805-RE3-3713) is located in Lompoc, nineteen miles west of U.S. Highway 101 from Buellton in a 966-acre Historical Park. A fiesta is held in May when all mission industries and activities are re-created. Open daily from 9:00 A.M. to 6:00 P.M., the mission is closed to tourists on Thanksgiving, Christmas, and New Year's Day. Group tours can be arranged.

Stone effigies in the area tell us that the Chumash Indians might have occupied the low hills south of the Santa Inez River seven thousand years before the Franciscan padres arrived.

Father Lasuén approved of the chosen site and named the mission in Spanish the Mission of the Immaculate Conception of the Most Holy Mary.

The docile and industrious Indians, the rich loam of the valley soil, and the mild weather, combined to bring joy to the hearts of the padres; for within five months after the first crude buildings were begun, seventy-five neophytes had been baptized. The mission did not prosper as the years passed.

Finally, in 1804, Padre Mariano Payeras, whose religious zeal was matched only by his insight into practical matters, arrived to head the mission. The padre knew that the other nearby missions were thriving, with orchards and gardens of wheat, corn, peas, beans, grapes, pears, peaches and other fruit. But not La Purísima. The difficulty was an inadequate water system. Father Payeras immediately devised one which was reputed to be a marvel of mechanical ingenuity. Even the drinking water was filtered through three feet of charcoal and sand.

61

The mission seemed fated for ill fortune. After 1804, though the granaries began to fill and the mission trade to prosper, dreaded diseases such as smallpox, measles, and others began to enlarge the cemeteries for the neophytes. A black pall of fear hung over the daytime rituals of work, crafts, and games. The La Purísima Indians had taken enormous pride in the perfection of the woolen blankets and cotton materials woven on the eight mission looms; but many of the weavers now fled to the hills and once again warmed themselves with deer hides. They could neither understand nor accept the beginnings of the annihilation of their race.

But there was further dread yet to be injected into the hearts of the neophytes, for, midmorning on December 21, 1812, while Father Payeras and his cohorts were inspecting the mission buildings, a violent earthquake shook the very foundations of the mission for over four minutes, it was said. Then, heavy rains tore at the exposed adobe, and the buildings fell into such disrepair that they were never restored to their former appearance.

After the earthquake, utility and strength became the bywords in building La Purísima. Beauty would take even less than second place. The church measured three hundred feet by fifty feet. The fathers' residence hall was buttressed with stone, its walls four and one-half feet thick. Its colonnade, one of the finest in the mission system, had twenty fluted columns under a low-sweeping tile roof.

Through all these difficulties, Padre Payeras guided strongly and wisely. When he died in 1823, the mission neophytes were lost.

A third disaster was to effectively stop further development of the mission. The next year an Indian revolt, which had started at Santa Inés, spread to La Purísima. It did not arrive unheralded. A new power structure had gradually seeped into the mission life. The burden of supporting the soldiery fell upon the Indians, a responsibility which they highly resented. On one occasion when an Indian at Santa Inés was flogged, the news was carried, post haste, by messenger to the neophytes at La Purísima, and, by three o'clock that afternoon, the Indians had revolted, seizing the mission. Here, the Indians held control for nearly thirty days, and were finally dispatched by Governor Arguello, who, aided by his troops, battered away at the mission wall with muskets and a four-pounder. Another detachment encircled the entire mission area.

This event marked the end of the docility of the Indians; and even though the crops and tallow and other supplies were still plentiful, fewer Indians chose to live and work on the mission grounds.

Helen Hunt Jackson, in her book, *Glimpses of California and the Missions,* published in 1883, wrote dramatically of the La Purísima Mission:

> "The painted pulpit hangs half falling on the wall, its stairs are gone, and its sounding board is slanting awry. Inside the broken altar rail is a pile of stones, earth, and rubbish thrown up by seekers after buried treasures; in the farther corner another pile and hole, the home of a badger; mud swallows' nests are thick on the cornice, and cobwebbed rags of the old canvas ceiling hang fluttering overhead. . . ."

Disintegration of the mission continued until 1935, when the 507-acre tract became a state monument with an increased size of 980 acres. Great care was taken by the C.C.C. laborers and craftsmen who performed the restoration. That "bugging" sense of pride, and the striving for an outstanding job were said to be the feelings of the workmen. This major project was begun in

Carreta used at La Purísima by the Indians.

1936 and finally ended with the interior decoration of the church. The day the mission was opened to the public was, indeed, an historic one; it was December 7, 1941, the morning of the attack on Pearl Harbor.

Each of the furnishings in the Mission La Purísima—whether a chandelier of gilded cast-brass, a mahogany bench, a tin mirror, or a chair made of fruitwood—is a precise replica of pieces at the other missions. In the chapel, there are no seats and worshippers must kneel on the floor.

The La Purísima Mission, sometimes called the "Williamsburg of the West," is now preserved under the California State Park System, with the consequent good fortune of being able to draw from the government continuous care, restoration, and even some of its former usefulness.

Mission San Luis Obispo de Tòlosa.

IO MISSION SAN LUIS OBISPO DE TÒLOSA (1772)

Mission San Luis Obispo de Tòlosa (805-543-1034) is at the corner of Monterey and Chorro Streets in San Luis Obispo on U.S. Highway 101. Group tours are arranged upon request and it is open daily from 6:30 A.M. to 5:30 P.M., except for Thanksgiving, Christmas, and New Year's Day.

The bears were a deciding factor in the Indians' acceptance of the padres in this locale. The natives here had an innate fear of the bears, as they could not kill them with their arrows; they felt a grudging admiration for the men who could vanquish these beasts of the forests.

In the valley that the Indians called Tixlini and the Spaniards called Canada de los Osos, the Valley of the Bears, Father Serra founded the Mission San Luis Obispo de Tòlosa, in honor of Saint Louis of Toulouse, France. It was September 1, 1772.

But the early days were difficult. On three different occasions, the unfriendly Indians shot burning wicks into the *tule* roofs of the early mission buildings. Instead of being defeated, the padres retaliated with a countermeasure by using tiles baked in an oven until they were a deep red.

Building then went onward at San Luis Obispo at a nice rate until the quadrangle was completed by 1819. Walter Colton, the first American Alcalde of Monterey, described the thriving opulence of the mission under the shrewd guidance of Father Luis Anthonio Martinez:

"He planted the cotton tree, the lime, and a grove of olives, which still shower their abundant harvest on

67

the tables of Californians. He built a launch that ran to Santa Barbara, trained his Indians to kill the otter, and often received thirty to forty skins a week from his children of the bow."

Historians tell us that Father Martinez was tough, brave, and jovial. But, according to Miss Jackson, Father Martinez was a bit eccentric. She cites the occasion when the father held a celebration for the Mexican General Moreno and his bride. All the mission poultry were driven by the onlookers, a procession that took the better part of an hour. Perhaps the father had special reasons to be proud of the feathered members of his flock.

Father Luis was no ecclesiastic to hide within the portals of the mission. When Argentine pirates attacked the coastline of California, the elderly padre left his sickbed, marched his neophytes to Santa Barbara, and prepared for battle. As the marauders were not to be found there, Father Luis, not to be daunted one whit by an elusive enemy, continued his trek as far down as San Juan Capistrano, all the while lamenting that he could do much better if he had two cannons.

Father Martinez was not universally appreciated, however. Father Luis' dislike for bureaucracy was a thorn in the flesh of the pompous, cock-of-the-roost Governor Echeandía, who forthwith arrested the padre on a charge of treason, gave him an illegal court martial, and banished him to Spain.

Besides the hurried return of their greatest supporter to Spain, the residents of San Luis Obispo also were oppressed by bandits, especially the infamous Murrieta and his men, who spent several days camping on the mission grounds and sleeping in store lofts nearby. Soon after, Murrieta was reported to have been captured by a California Ranger, in a canyon near Coalinga, for a bounty of $1,000. Murrieta's head—or that of some luckless Mexican—was pickled in a jar of alcohol and displayed in a San

Francisco Barbary Coast saloon. It was destroyed in the earthquake and fire of 1906, but not until thousands of morbid sightseers had paid $1.00 each to see it.

The mission bell was noticeably quiet at the supposed death of Murrieta. An interesting side note to history is that the actual ringing of the bells was considered a sought-after position by the neophytes. Many of the bell-ringers at the missions have made history, as has Gregorio Silverio who, for more than fifty years, tolled the bells at Mission San Luis Obispo.

According to Pauline Bradley, a writer of California history, Gregorio had been taught by a ninety-year-old Indian. This teacher, Florentine Naja, had cautioned his young protegé, "Go slow or you'll crack the bells. Don't make a ding-dong like a cow bell. Make a mellow tone that sings."

Gregorio was proud that he had rung the bells for over 3,000 funerals, for the deaths of popes, presidents, and bishops, and for Edison and Will Rogers.

Gregorio died in 1954, but, with rare farsightedness, before his death he had taught his granddaughter, Virginia Lee White, the intricate patterns and "touch" of the bells. Virginia, in turn, has been teaching other townspeople the proper position in which to stand, the rhythm, and the light touch. Most importantly, the beauty of the bell-ringing has been perpetuated.

All three of the original bells are inscribed and are named the Angelus, the Joyful, and the Sorrowful.

By 1834, a few years after Father Martinez's departure, the mission, its grounds, and its cattle were valued at $70,000. In 1845, sadly, all but the cattle was sold at public auction for $510, and the mission became a courthouse-townhall-school.

Restoration began, to a degree, in 1847, when Father Garcia enclosed the crumbling buildings with sturdy clapboard and added a wooden cupola. Those with an artistic eye claimed that the lovely appearance of the mission had been lost. Almost a

A view through the covered walkway at San Luis Obispo.

century later, in 1935, more serious and extensive restoration took place, and today the courtyard, the church, and the priests' quarters very closely resemble those of more than 150 years ago; unhappily, there is no trace of the quadrangle with its memories of neophytes spinning, forging, and weaving in closely knit groups, or of children playing a game resembling our football.

Today, visitors to San Luis Obispo notice the attractively landscaped plaza, designed by the students at California Polytechnic State University, with assistance from the local citizens, and replete with footbridges, shops and restaurants. Altogether, the mission is considered one of the showplaces of the state.

*Bell tower separated by mission compound at
Mission San Miguel Arcángel.*

II MISSION SAN MIGUEL ARCÁNGEL
(1797)

Mission San Miguel Arcángel (805-467-3256) can be found in the town of San Miguel on old U.S. Highway 101, nine miles north of Paso Robles. Used as a monastery and retreat for people of all faiths, the mission has an annual fiesta on the third Sunday of September and celebrates La Posadas in December. It is open daily from 10:00 A.M. to 5:00 P.M.

The Mission San Miguel Arcángel faces the King's Highway, or El Camino Real, a road that accommodated the old creaking *carretas* of the Californios, as well as the compact cars of today.

The site, in the midst of pine-covered hills, was chosen by Father Lasuén, who was then Presidente of the Mission Chain, and the mission was named after the Prince of the Heavenly Militia. Even on that first founding day, fifteen Indian children were offered for baptism. The date was July 25, 1797, the feast day of St. James the Apostle.

This mission lacked many of the features of the other missions. The soil was not so fertile, nor the weather as temperate. Disaster hit in 1806, when a fire damaged the workrooms, the granaries, and the church roof.

By 1818, the present mission was started. The plans were simple, with a nave 144 feet long and an unembellished exterior. Contrary to the custom then, there was no bell tower. After years of quakes, the padres were now determined to establish a solid structure, with walls six feet thick—the length of an extra-tall neophyte. And, today, the original roof stands intact and is spanned by beams of Monterey sugar pine, hand cut with an adze by the Indians, who brought these woods from the Santa Lucia Mountains, some forty miles distant to the west.

Years later, in 1821, the padres, bending to the dictates of their artistic souls, engaged the Spanish artist Estéban Munras to paint the decorations on the walls and ceilings of the church.

The Indians had experimented already with paints—the blue from the wild flowers, the red from certain rocks, the bright dyes mixed with glue made from the bones of cattle. These, Munras used with great skill and good fortune; for the paintings have never needed to be retouched in the century and a half that has passed since he painted them.

The following year, in 1822, the mission owned 91,000 head of cattle, 1,100 tame horses, 3,000 mares, 2,000 mules, 170 yoke of working oxen, and 47,000 sheep. Astounding numbers! It was a prosperous operation.

Like most of the other missions, San Miguel was sold at auction, and a Mr. Guillermo Reed, a cattle and sheep raiser as well as a merchant for the miners from the San Joaquin Valley, was recorded as the owner in 1849. Reed was a practical joker and finally one evening his brand of amusement boomeranged. He had been in the habit of telling visitors to the mission long (and probably tall) tales of bags of gold dust and nuggets hidden away. One night, a party of four white men and an Indian guide, who later left because of ill treatment, stopped by, heard Reed's story, and then proceeded to axe the merchant rancher to death, along with those in his household. It was a grim ending to what seemed a harmless enough pastime, creative story telling.

The incident was scandalous, but not unusual in this region where spring roundups often triggered a murder or two in a local saloon in Creston or Estrella.

The mission lay in almost complete ruins, from the late 1800s on, until, in 1923, the Franciscan padres returned to San

74

Miguel. Once again, the gardens became fragrant with flowers and the old fountain was restored.

In the early 1930s, Father Tibertius Wand, a native Bavarian, came to San Miguel. The Indians grew to love him and called him Father Juan. The father had a thick accent, which caused great humor among his parishioners, despite their high respect for him. Natives in town recall the morning when an Indian buck started teasing a lady seated in front of him during mass by tipping her glasses. Father Juan grabbed the mischievous Indian by the seat of his trousers, threw him out of the church, calling out, "Zen I finish my sermon on batience!"

Today, San Miguel is fortunate to have many priceless art treasures—the old, old paintings in muted oils, and the three statues, of Saint Michael, Saint Francis, and Saint Anthony, in the panels behind the altar.

In 1888, six cracked and broken bells, collected from other missions, were recast into one huge 2,500 pounder. In the 1950s, this bell was moved to a little *companario* at the rear of the church.

The original wall-pulpit is a thing of beauty done in rich colors of scarlet, blue, silver; and there is the Wishing Chair, where Father Magín Catalá, when visiting the mission, gave a blessing and promised a maiden that, if she sat there, she would have her heart's desire.

The mission church still reflects the days of the neophytes— the decorations in red, blue, pink, and two shades of green, with motifs of leaves and tassels. The rafters, all twenty-eight of them, were each rough-hewn from a single tree. Cut at Cambria, they were transported across the rough terrain of the Santa Lucia Mountains.

Today, the young Franciscan priests who live at the Mission San Miguel, maintain the mission as a parish church and monastery.

75

Mission San Antonio de Padua.

12 MISSION SAN ANTONIO DE PADUA (1771)

Mission San Antonio de Padua (408-385-4478) is located just off U.S. Highway 101, twenty-three miles southwest of King City. This mission celebrates a fiesta and barbecue in June and has special ceremonies on Christmas Eve to which the public is invited. It is open from 9:00 A.M. to 4:30 P.M. Monday through Saturday, and from 11:00 A.M. to 5:00 P.M. on Sunday.

The Mission San Antonio de Padua was the first mission to have an Indian present at its founding. No doubt he was attracted by the bell hung from a tree and rung vigorously by Father Serra. San Antonio was situated in the Valley of the Oaks, in 1771, and dedicated to the "Miracle Worker," St. Anthony de Padua, in whose honor the first mass was celebrated.

The Indians here were well fed; the adjacent hills offered wild game and pheasant, turkey, and grouse. The natives ground their own coarse flour from the acorns, and though the resulting bread was described by visitors as "quite heavy," the diet had proved nourishing. With alacrity, the Indians offered to help the padres float the timbers down the San Antonio River. A mill race and a water wheel were built.

The first buildings were completed by 1773, but not until many years later, in 1810, was the large church built. Father Sitjar, who served at San Antonio for thirty-seven years, devised a marvelous system of dams, aqueducts, and reservoirs. His engineering skill is evidenced by the irrigation ditches still used by the ranchers in the area.

The mission thrived, and the grist mill, running at full speed, produced a flour much superior to the Indian meal. The ranchos became famous for the golden-colored Palomino horses which, even then, were the favorites for parades and fiestas. The author Reisenberg tells us that at San Antonio the neophytes proudly invited their friends to stay overnight so they could hear the "long gowns" sing the Canticle of Dawn.

As the years passed into the pastoral period, *vaqueros* were apt to stop at the mission for prayers or for the celebration of the mass, as they drove their rangy, black, Spanish cattle over the route behind the mission, which led through Reliz Canyon and down into the Salinas Valley.

Nearby the mission is Priest Valley, which was rather strangely but appropriately named by the famous explorer and Indian scout, Kit Carson. The story goes that Carson and his partner, Captain Joe Walker, were searching for pasture for their live-stock and climbed out of the valley and into the hills. There they discovered a priest kneeling in prayer—Padre Doroteo Ambris from the Mission San Antonio—and so the name was recorded.

Decay set in and, by 1852, Father Ambris, a Mexican Indian reared from childhood by the padres and ordained a priest at Santa Barbara, was sent to guard the mission. For thirty years he worked there, indulging his special fondness for the flower and vegetable gardens.

In the 1870s, the novelist Gertrude Atherton wrote of the pathetic picture of the Mission San Antonio:

> "The women were very fat [speaking of the fifty-three families crowded into the mission] wearing a solitary calico garment and the children, although the San Antonio Valley is bitter cold in winter, quite naked."

78

From the very early 1900s, the mountains around the mission were a favorite haunt for commercial hunters, who sold the game to fine restaurants in San Francisco.

In 1903, festooned horses and buggies, with riders in a gala mood, congregated at the ruins of the mission. Their intention was not only merry-making, but the beginning of the project to restore the mission. Several other attempts were made later, but it was not until 1948, with a grant from the Hearst Foundation, that the work was begun in earnest.

Wiped out by European diseases, so few people of native Indian ancestry survived that, by 1950, Dolores Encinal, a San Antonio Indian, was a figure of note to be pointed out to visitors as he walked about King City wearing his old hat with its high crown. His father had been a courier at the mission and he himself had been a cowboy. A few of the Indians lived to a very old age, such as the squaw Lupesina of the Mission San Antonio, who died at 116 and had shrunk to the height of a mere four feet.

Today, a delightful *campanario* stands unique among the bell walls of the mission chain. Behind it lies a barrel vault that leads into the church itself. The restored interior of the church is muted in color and is pleasant to the eyes.

Perhaps, due in part, at least, to the fact that only two owners—William Randolph Hearst and the U.S. Army—held title to the vast tract of land surrounding the mission since the days of secularization, the pastoral setting has been kept intact.

Crumbling ruins of original mission with completed restoration of Mission Nuestra Señora de la Soledad in background.

13 MISSION NUESTRA SEÑORA DE LA SOLEDAD (1791)

The Soledad Mission (408-678-2586) is located off U.S. Highway 101, three miles south and one mile west of Soledad. Its annual fiesta is held around September 29 and it is open from 10:00 A.M. to 4:30 P.M. Tuesday through Sunday.

Shakespeare asked, "What's in a name?" And indeed the name chosen for the Mission Nuestra Señora Dolorisima, Our Most Sorrowful Lady of Solitude, may well have had a serious portent. From its very beginnings, when Father Fermín Francisco Lasuén founded the site, which was chosen as a needed stopover between Carmel and San Antonio de Padua, the mission lived up to its name of Soledad, which means loneliness.

About a mile west of the nearby Salinas River was the famous "upside-down" stream (most of its flow of water was underground and unseen by summertime) surrounded by almost treeless and sunbaked hills and plains.

Yet, Soledad must have flourished during the years around the first of the century, for 2,234 baptisms are on the mission records.

There was little that could be considered auspicious about this particular mission. The plagues had a frightening effect upon the Indians and many escaped into the hills and back to their pagan way of life. The rains, often prayed for during the hot, dry periods, were more apt to be heavy sheet floods that washed away the adobe buildings. The chilling dampness of the adobe buildings caused the padres to suffer with rheumatism. And it did not take much persuasion for the fathers to try the soothing mud baths in the hot sulphur springs a few miles from the mission. Here the

81

Indians (and grizzlies!) had bathed for years and had drunk the mineral water brought up by large mills which are still standing. The therapeutic value of the waters might be vouchsafed by the tale of an Indian named Gabriel who, in 1890, was said to be the oldest living human in the world—150 years of age, with hair as black as tar, and still living on the mission grounds.

As the years passed, the plight of those remaining after secularization at the Mission Soledad was one of misery and sadness. No longer could the fathers operate their centers of agriculture and industry. The Mexican government, by one means or another, had drained all the mission's resources.

Padre Sarria, faithful to the few remaining neophytes, made trips on foot to the surrounding settlers, pleading for donations of food and money. Quite simply, he told of the small Indian children that were slowly starving, how many of the older Indians had died, and how others had left to find work in the *presidios*. Apparently the Americanos had forgotten the favors of the mission fathers, for Sarria's quests were fruitless.

As food grew more scarce, Padre Sarria's health began to fail. A messenger was sent to bring Jesus Maria Vasquez del Mercado, the priest who alone was caring for the Mission San Antonio. But, before he could arrive, Padre Sarria slumped at the altar as he was delivering mass on a Sunday morning. Indians carried his body to San Antonio and it was interred at the right of the altar near the wall of the chapel.

Finally, in 1846, the mission was sold by the governor for $800; and, although the church regained the property in 1859, the mission was not reactivated for ninety years.

Feliciano Soberanes bought the mission property in 1847. It was still a lonely place. In fact a visitor in 1849 reported, "a more desolate place than Soledad cannot well be imagined . . . not a tree or a shrub is to be seen anywhere in the vicinity."

82

Under the decree of President Buchanan, in November, 1859, forty-two acres, including the church buildings and dwellings, gardens, orchards, vineyards, and cemeteries, were patented to Archbishop Alemany.

Years later, in 1954, with only small remains of adobe to mark the mission site, restoration was begun. For 117 years, the Mission Soledad had stood in ruins; even the floor was discovered three feet below the ground's surface.

With the energetic help of the Native Daughters of the Golden West, a chapel has been built on the opposite side of the quadrangle from the site of the first church. And the original paintings of the fourteen Stations of the Cross, fortunately preserved at the Carmel and San Antonio Missions, are hanging inside the chapel.

Twelve thousand adobe bricks, taken from the dust of the disintegrated buildings, were made as part of the restoration. Another 20,000 were needed for the West Wing. The adobe bricks were molded in the old mission way and sun-dried. No effort has seemed too costly to bring back a faithful reproduction of the Mission Soledad.

Mission San Carlos Borromeo de Carmelo.

14 MISSION SAN CARLOS BORROMEO DE CARMELO (1770)

San Carlos (408-624-3600) is located south of Carmel near State Highway 1. The last Sunday in September the yearly fiesta in honor of St. Charles Borromeo is celebrated. Visitors are given a map of the grounds and a brief history of the mission, and they can then tour the grounds from 9:30 A.M. to 5:00 P.M. Monday through Saturday and from 10:30 A.M. to 5:00 P.M. on Sunday.

This story begins, not at the mouth of the Carmel River, but over the hill in Monterey, where Padre Serra met Gaspar de Portolá and his party of explorers on June 3, 1770. Father Serra built a temporary cabin where he worked as overseer and laborer, but first he ordered a large cross made which he raised and blessed.

Soon the general rowdiness of the party disturbed the padres. They were concerned about the influence of the military over the impressionable and imitative neophytes. Then, too, the soil nearer the river seemed more receptive to crops. So the move was made.

Life at the new mission was stark. Early in 1774, when the supply ship from Mexico was delayed for eight months, Anza, who visited the mission during that bleak time, reported that all its inhabitants went thirty-seven days without a tortilla or a crumb of bread; not even a small cake of chocolate was to be found.

Father Serra's cell had been most frugally furnished, as was his wish—just a cot of boards, a single blanket, a table and chair, a chest, a candlestick, and a gourd.

When death took the father in 1784, processions of mourners

85

trekked to the adobe church at the mission. There was a General's salute—the booming of a cannon off Monterey Bay, answered by the guns at the *presidio* and by the bells of the mission. Father Serra had confirmed 5,307 persons. He was tired and wanted to be buried beside his lifelong friend, Father Crespi. His last words were "Thanks be to God, now there is no fear, I will rest a little."

One of the first dealings the mission fathers had with the subjects of a foreign power was the visit, in 1786, of the navigator, Jean Francois Galaup de la Pérouse. Pérouse was on an exploring expedition for his king with a full entourage of scientific specialists. Entering Monterey Bay, he dropped anchor, but was dismayed at the whales that came within spouting distance of the ships. La Pérouse reported that he saw the fires of a volcano in the distance. Later this was disproved and found to be only the Indians setting fire to the grass in order to dry the pods of grain, which made them easier to gather.

Six years later the Mission San Carlos was to receive yet another distinguished visitor, the English explorer, Captain George Vancouver, whose ship *Discovery* lay in anchor while needed repairs were being made. A tent and an observatory for astronomical observations were set up on the beach while Vancouver and his officers found their way to the mission. Their welcome at San Carlos was most cordial. Vancouver described the country as "lively," the surface of the landscape as "an agreeable verdure." Archibald Menzies, who accompanied Vancouver, wrote of the Indian huts, "sometimes there are cushions for the women to sit down on and, if they take their seats before a stranger arrives, they never stir to pay the least homage to him."

Here, at Mission San Carlos, Serra, and his successors, set up headquarters as Father Presidente of the Missions. When Father Lasuén was in charge, the mission project had matured enough to give rise to charges of cruelty or unfairness on the part of the padres. The father worked diligently, with much concern, to ferret out the guilty parties and then to have them discharged.

The Indians left after the secularization and the mission was offered for sale. But there were no buyers; a fact almost unbelievable today in view of the incredibly high prices of adjacent land. Only one padre was left to care for the few remaining Indians. He was said to be a cheerful man who always carried apples in the sleeves of his robe for the children. One day this padre also left.

T. J. Farnham, in a book on his travels, sets the scene of the mission in 1841, after the secularization:

> "The whole structure is somewhat lofty, and looks down upon the surrounding scenery, like an old baronial castle. An oaken armchair, brown and marred with age, stood on the piazza, proclaiming to Our Lady of Guadaloupe and a group of saints rudely sketched upon the walls, that Carmelo was deserted by living men. . . ."

In 1882, Father Casanova cleared the grounds and began restoring the mission. Here was a superb setting of sea and mountains, perhaps the most romantically beautiful spot of the mission chain, but the restoration was abandoned and not renewed until the 1930s. It was completed during the 1950s. At that time, Father Serra's starkly bare and minuscule cell was carefully rebuilt.

Robert Louis Stevenson loved Monterey and, in "The Old Pacific Capital," he describes the fiesta at the Carmel Mission:

> "Only one day in the year . . . the padre drives over the hill from Monterey; the little sacristy, which is the only covered portion of the church is filled with seats

Handsome fountain at the Carmel Mission.

and decorated for the service; the Indians troop together, their bright dresses contrasting with their dark
and melancholy faces; and there, among a crowd of
somewhat unsympathetic holiday-makers, you may
hear God served with perhaps more touching circum-
stances than in any other temple under heaven."

Today, in the mortuary chapel stands the treasured statue of
the Virgin that Father Serra took with him to the founding of the
San Diego Mission. The star window and other Moorish architectural details were arranged by Father Lasuén.

As you enter the church, the first window you see on the opposite side was brought in on a "Boston ship"—as Alta Californians
always spoke of the American trading vessels, no matter what
the actual location of the home port.

A visitor to the Mission San Carlos is impressed with the love-
liness and beauty of things old and treasured, and that which is
still growing and being nurtured.

Mission San Juan Bautista.

15 MISSION SAN JUAN BAUTISTA
(1797)

This mission (408-623-4528) is found in the town of San Juan Bautista, four miles south of U.S. Highway 101 and seventeen miles north of Salinas. A rodeo and fiesta is held in July and another fiesta in honor of Our Lady of Guadalupe is celebrated in December. It is open daily from 9:00 A.M. to 5:00 P.M.

The Mission San Juan Bautista has mellowed in beauty and in the glory of continuous service for over 150 years. The setting is natural, Old California, and there is a feeling visitors enjoy that time has indeed paused here.

In 1797, on St. John's Day, June 24, Father Lasuén dedicated this mission "in the name of Jesus Christ, Our Lord, Saint John Baptist." Within three years there were 500 Indians living at the mission, in its fertile valley. When an earthquake in 1800 caused extensive damage, the padres decided to build another church. In 1803, a cornerstone was laid amid fitting ceremonies.

Then, in 1808, Father Felipe del Arroyo de la Cuesta, said to be a genius and a fortunate composite of learning, talent and imagination, arrived on the mission scene. Old plans for the church were soon tossed aside and a much grander one was initiated—no less than three aisles instead of the usual long narrow nave were planned.

Persistence might have been the slogan of the years, for it took fifteen years to build this church, the largest in the province; and the same floor tiles, with their imprints of mountain lions, and the four-foot-thick adobe walls still stand.

The grandeur of the plans, however, was not in keeping with the neophyte attendance that was rapidly decreasing in numbers;

91

and so the ingenious Father de la Cuesta walled in the two rows of arches that he had favored so highly. Now, again, the church was scaled down to the familiar mission type. Only two arches were left open, showing the magnificence of the padre's plan.

Later, the mission was to have a New England flavor, for Thomas Doak, a Yankee sailor who had jumped ship at Monterey and thereby earned the title of the first American citizen to settle in California, painted the altar. His artistry might have been of a dubious quality, but the paints, made of animal and vegetable dyes, have lasted through the years. A Mexican painter had tried to exploit the good fathers for six reales (75 cents) a day, but Doak was evidently so glad to be on dry land in a community of abundant food, that he decided against driving a shrewd Yankee bargain.

Not all of La Cuesta's energies were directed toward building, as the man was also a skillful linguist, with a command of over a dozen dialects, who could sermonize in any one of seven languages.

The mission was fortunate to have another remarkable priest, Father Estévan Tapis, former acting Presidente of the Missions. His was a musical talent of note, and, on huge sheets of sheepskin (each page required one sheep), he painted large square notes of black, red, yellow and green. In this way, an Indian singer need only follow the notes of a certain color. He formed a choir of Indian boys who were well known.

One day, a band of warring Tulare Indians frightened the mission Indians, who swiftly ran for cover. But Father Tapis, with what he no doubt referred to as "divine" inspiration, made for the barrel organ. The neophytes rallied enough to sing along even though they didn't know the words; and the hostile Tulares

View of Mission looking across only remaining Spanish Plaza in California.

stood transfixed to listen. In fact, they found the music so fascinating that they decided to remain at the mission.

In the latter half of the nineteenth century, functional utility seemed to be the order of the day, with beauty and artistry lagging behind. And, in this vein, a wooden tower was affixed to the church in 1860 and later duplicated in concrete. The architecture did not harmonize, but at least the church bells could be rung in comfort, even in inclement weather. Only one of the original bells remains at the mission, but it can still be heard eight miles across the valley.

If a mission escaped large damage in the great temblor of 1812, it seemed that another earthquake was preparing itself to take its toll. In 1906, the church was so damaged by a quake, that gaping holes in the side walls resulted and, in fact, still remain.

In 1849, a traveler wrote of the mission lands:

> "Its fertility is enough to make a New England plow jump out of its rocks; a hundred emigrants will yet squat in its green bosom and set the wild Indians and their warhoop at defiance."

San Juan Bautista, as with many other missions, was drawn into the tight net of battle between the United States and Mexico. In 1846, General José Castro, Commandante of all the Mexican forces in California, summoned reinforcements at San Juan Batista. For three days, the troops tried to scale Gavilan Peak, where John C. Fremont and his men built a log cabin and raised the American flag, but to no avail. No battle ensued, and perhaps this occasion gave rise to the familiar expression "a Mexican standoff."

A New Yorker, William H. Brewer, taking a geological survey of California from 1860 to 1868, wrote in his journal:

> ". . . a congregation of perhaps 150-200 knelt, sat, or stood on its brick floor—a mixed and motley throng, but devout—Mexican, Indian, mixed breeds, Irish, French, German. . . . It is only in a Roman church that one sees such a picturesque mingling of races, so typical of Christian brotherhood."

Mission San Juan Bautista is still an active parish church and a picnic area is provided for visitors.

Front view of replica of Mission Santa Cruz.

16 MISSION SANTA CRUZ (1791)

Mission Santa Cruz (408-426-5686) is located on Emmet and School Streets in Santa Cruz. It is open daily from 9:00 A.M. to 5:00 P.M. and tours can be arranged in advance.

The fate of the *original* Mission Santa Cruz is a strange one, for not a vestige remains. A historical landmark sign records the site, while a block away a dainty replica of the original, one-half its size, has been built using old sketches and paintings.

This was an auspicious site, or so it seemed to Father Crespi as he journeyed through with Portola in 1769. Padres Palou and Lasuén, who selected it for the twelfth mission, were equally impressed. Grasses and berries grew richly, game could be sighted within musket range, and pine and redwood trees covered the nearby mountains.

Within three years, the church stood on a rise near the San Lorenzo River, looking out on the Bay with a forest in the background. The building was of good size, 30 feet wide and 112 feet long. The front was built of masonry, the three-foot foundation was of stone, and the rest of the structure was adobe.

The early years at the mission were good, but they were numbered. There was an abundance of water, timber, and building stone, and even shells for the making of lime. The growth of the fruits and vegetables was outsized in this fertile soil, and for years the whalers who ran into Monterey stocked their holds with these fresh edibles from the mission of the Holy Cross.

Late in 1794, Vancouver visited the mission fathers. He

97

badly needed the fresh green vegetables to prevent the dreaded scurvy among his crew. And, with a typical show of gratitude, he presented the mission with ironwork for a gristmill. It took two years for the mill to become fully operable, but it was highly prized by neophytes and padres alike.

The history of the mission might have been different were it not for Branciforte. This was a name that brought misery to the hearts of the mission padres. At first, the plan had seemed to have merit—a pueblo located just across the river from the mission and named for the Viceroy of Mexico, the Marqués de Branciforte. A town was laid out with neat white houses for the colonists. And, to round out the package, annual bonuses were promised the men, in addition to clothes, farm tools, and furniture.

But it was a two-way disappointment. About seventeen settlers arrived to find no houses built, only meager huts. On the other side of the coin, the newcomers were lawless, indolent, and thoroughly undesirable; and they pressed their luck by vying with the padres over pasture lands and the labor of the Indians.

That was the state of affairs when news reached the mission that the privateer Bouregard had been spotted off Monterey Bay. The fathers were ordered to pack up, and take with them, all valuables. The pirates did not land at the Santa Cruz side of the bay, but the residents of Branciforte quite made up for this with their own pillaging and looting.

The years slowly passed. In 1806, with a great deal of satisfaction, the padres put a gristmill into operation to grind the grains stored in the mission granaries. The millhouse was two-storied, with the water wheel in the lower part and the millstones and storeroom above.

1812 was a year of sorrow for the mission. Father Quintana was found dead in his bed one morning. There was little conjecture as to the cause, as the padre had been in ill health for some time. So, the good Father rested in peace until rumors of murder led to an investigation. Then it was learned that Father Quintana had been out of his bed the night of his demise to attend a dying man. On the way home, he was set upon and brutally murdered. He was placed in bed afterward and the door locked. Only one of the guilty neophytes survived the punishment, and the autopsy was the first in California history.

The herds continued to increase at Santa Cruz, the crops flourished, but the number of Indians at the mission dwindled, perhaps due to the influence of the Branciforte colony or because of its isolated location, off the main highway that ran from Monterey to San Francisco. Away from the fatherly guidance of the padres, the Indian *vaqueros* frequented Whiskey Hill, a place where every rickety shack was a saloon.

The secularization in 1834 had the same ill effect on this mission as it did on many others. The lands fell into the hands of strangers and, four years later, only a sixth of the parcels listed could be located.

A severe quake in 1840 shattered the church, and, by 1846, there was so little left to sell that not even the enterprising Governor Pio Pico found anything of interest. Yet the church withstood the ravages of new settlers until, in 1840, an earthquake was followed by a mammoth tidal wave, which tore away the tower and broke many of the tiles. In 1851, the weakened walls fell and the mission lay totally in ruins.

In 1857, the old church caved in with such a resounding crash that the entire village was awakened. Today, the half-scale replica, erected in 1932 with funds donated by Mrs. Gladys Sullivan Doyle, is a favorite chapel for weddings and private services.

Mission Santa Clara de Asis.

17 MISSION SANTA CLARA DE ASIS (1777)

This mission (408-984-4242) is located on the campus of Santa Clara University. It is open from 9:00 A.M. to 5:00 P.M.

A rich and lush meadowland was chosen for the site of the Mission Santa Clara de Asis, dedicated to Mother Ste. Claire of Assisi, Spiritual Sister of St. Francis and Holy Matriarch of his order. The date was January 12, 1777, the place, the southern end of San Francisco Bay.

Amazingly, the mission still resembles, to a great degree, the original edifice designed and built by the talented Father Murguiá; the resemblance exists despite three changes in site, and five demolitions by earthquake and fire. The first site was endangered by the flood waters of the Alviso and Guadalupe Rivers. Finally, in 1781, the cornerstone of Father Murguiá's church was laid near Santa Clara's present railway station. The father, after laboring to erect the most beautiful and elaborate church in California up to that time, lived only to see its completion. He died four days before it was dedicated by Father Serra.

Santa Clara's church buildings were to undergo many changes, including those forced upon them by an earthquake in 1818. A third set of buildings some distance from the original site, which were completed in 1825, served the parishioners until two wooden churches were substituted. These buildings later were razed by fire.

Nearby was the Pueblo San José, a constant irritation to the mission fathers because the settlers on this first civil settlement in California were inclined to encroach on the mission lands, which

101

lacked formal boundaries. Also, they generally ignored the fathers' Sunday Mass.

So, Father Catala, using the old mountain-to-Mohammed theory, decided to link the mission to San José by a wide and beautiful tree-lined section of El Camino Real called the Alameda. He employed two hundred Indians to plant three rows of black willow trees (one row on each side of the road and one row in the middle) so that travelers would not have to walk in the hot summer sun. (Later, this middle row was removed to allow for horse cars in 1868, an electric omnibus system, and a steam railway in 1870.) Sadly, only three of the original willows remain.

The mission had one unfortunate Indian attack. Chief Yozcolo was the daring chief of a band of renegade Indians. During one of his most ambitious raids on the missions San José and Santa Clara, he and his band confiscated over 2,000 horses and a group of Indian girls. Straightway, the fathers sent word to Monterey—troops were to be paid a $2.00 bonus each to find the treacherous chief. Finally, Yozcolo was killed, and his head was left to rot on a pole over the Santa Clara Mission.

Father José Viader, who, with Father Catala, administered the mission for thirty-seven years, was a huge, powerful man with a heart that was equally immense. One night in 1814, the padre was attacked by a young Indian giant named Marcelo and two companions. Father Viader ended up thrashing his three assailants by himself. Then, after lecturing them soundly, he forgave them and later claimed Marcelo as one of his most faithful friends.

Father Viader, no doubt hankering for a bit of old-world grandeur coupled with a speedier mode of transportation, constructed the most luxurious vehicle of mission times. Surely no Rolls Royce had as much loving care as this narrow-bodied coach, which hung low and was hitched to a black mule. The single seat was stuffed with lamb's wool and brown cloth was stretched to cover the frame. The procession of the vehicle was eye-catching, to say the least. A small Indian boy sat on the mule which, in turn, was guided by a *vaquero* on horseback with two more *vaqueros* guarding each side of the coach and watching closely for the right moment to throw a *reata* around the axletree if Father Viader decided to drive up a steep hill.

Another well-known community figure was Father Catala. Called El Profeta (the prophet), he amazed his audiences by foretelling future happenings, such as the coming of the Americans, the discovery of gold, the loss of California by Spain, and the San Francisco earthquake of 1906.

In 1851, Father John Nobili was sent by the Society of Jesus to begin a university in the old mission buildings. This learned Jesuit padre taught with admirable simplicity, sitting on a tree trunk in the garden with the first twelve students on wooden benches under the grapevines. In this way, the College of Santa Clara, later the University of Santa Clara, was founded.

A grandiose plan for the college was published in a county atlas in 1870—the plan called for building a classic-styled campus around the old adobe mission. Today, Santa Clara University is recognized for its high-level sports and athletic programs, and its law and business schools. In the gardens are an original Castilian rosebush and the oldest grapevine in Northern California. This vine is shaped in the form of a crucifix.

At dusk, the bells in the new church, which was built in 1926 as a replica of the original mission, are faithfully rung. In the early days of the mission, the King sent two bells by the ship *San Antonio* to Monterey which were then loaded on oxcarts for the journey overland to Santa Clara. These bells celebrated the continuous activity of the Roman Catholic Church at this beautiful site for almost two hundred years.

Mission San José de Guadalupe.

18 MISSION SAN JOSÉ DE GUADALUPE (1797)

Mission San José (408-656-9125) is in Fremont at State High-
way 238 and Washington Boulevard. It has a historical museum
and is open daily from 10:00 A.M. to 4:30 P.M.

The founding of the Mission San José de Guadalupe was based
on a somewhat different premise than that of the other missions.
For several years, the Indians of the San Joaquin Valley, unlike
the more southern tribes, had great hostility toward the caravans
of people and goods that plied up and down the coast.

Father Fermin Lasuén, in addition to his other mental and
spiritual attributes, had the strategic mind of the diplomat. He
knew that the Spanish king's governor, Borica, was not keen on
spending more money to set up another mission. After all, it was
six years since the founding of Mission Soledad. Lasuén ap-
proached the Governor with the appeal that money could be
saved that was being spent on military equipment and supplies if
the Indians could be baptized and converted into peaceful neophytes. The Governor's answer was far more encouraging than
Lasuén had even dared to hope for—the Mission San José was
approved.

The founding day, according to the diarists, was a bright summer morning on June 11, 1797. By now, the padres from the
other missions were taking a brotherly stance. A group of the
fathers arrived with picnic hampers of dried beef rolled in tor-
tillas, cheese, candied fruits, and tea. They approved of the
chosen site at the bottom of beautiful Mission Peak. There was
even a sparkling view of the bay. The visitors returned to the
Mission Santa Clara still filled with interest and generosity toward
the infant mission.

Interior of chapel at Mission San José.

Sergeant Amador ordered his soldiers to assemble building materials and equipment. And, in less than two months, the newcomers at San José had a priest's room, a storehouse, soldiers' barracks, and a guard house. Missions Carmel and Dolores also gave fine gifts of food and stock. The climax to these happy beginnings came one morning late in the summer when a loud rumbling sound echoed throughout the valley. This was not one of the feared *temblores*. Instead, in a veritable haze of dust, a large herd of cattle, horses, and mules were being driven by the *vaqueros* from the Santa Clara Mission. When a flock of sheep arrived, some were slaughtered and barbecued amidst general rejoicing.

In the early 1800s, von Langsdorff Aulic, Counselor to the Emperor of Russia, visited the Mission San José. He felt that, although there were few large trees in the area, the chalk hills would make excellent bricks to compensate for the lack of wood.

He watched, with great interest, the Indians preparing for a native dance by smearing their bodies with charcoal dust, red clay, and chalk, or by covering their torsos with down feathers.

Perhaps due to the cold climate at San José, the Indians seemed especially eager to wear the new types of mission clothing—the woolen trousers and shirts, with ponchos for the *vaqueros*. Before the padres' arrival, the natives had worn the furs of animals or, if these were not available, they would cake themselves with mud from head to foot.

For over eight years, no outward signs of hostility from these Indians occurred. And so, the mission padres were beginning to relax when Padre Cueva was sent on a sick call to some neophyte Indians a good way from the mission compound. Two soldiers, a few Indians, and the majordomo comprised the party. Whether it was a trap, or other tribes of the hostile East Bay Indians were involved, no one seems to know for certain, but

Traditional covered walkway at Mission San José.

all except the padre were killed, and he was seriously injured.

Father Narcisco Duran was Presidente of the Missions and a strong, talented administrator. From 1806, and for the next twenty years, he brought brilliant leadership to the Mission San José. His forté was music, and, although he had had no professional background, he put together a choir and a thirty-five piece Indian orchestra. The neophytes learned to play the flute, violin, trumpet, and drums, and woe to a singer or player who hit a discordant note, for the padre was apt to reprimand him on the spot.

However, even peaceful years could be misleading. Father Duran was surprised and shocked one day in 1828 to learn that his trusted chieftain, Estanislao, had run away and was heading a band of marauders. The Indians were captured by General Mariano Vallejo, but the padre's disappointment was, no doubt, very keen.

Secularization came, and one of the late *alcaldes* of San Francisco wrote in 1846 of his visit to the nearby deserted Mission San José:

> ". . . nothing of moving life was visible except a donkey or two, standing near a fountain which gushed its waters into a capacious stone trough . . . filth and desolation were everywhere."

During the Gold Rush Days, the mission was converted into a trading post which grew rich crops to sell the miners.

The first mission church, which was dedicated in 1809, was later ravaged by the 1868 earthquake and had to be demolished. Not long after, the present wooden church was built upon the same site, and can be seen today looking rather pristine and dignified in appearance. In the rear of the church is an old grove of olive trees reminiscent of the patio workshop days, when the oil was needed for the altar lamps.

Mission San Francisco de Asís.

19 MISSION SAN FRANCISCO DE ASÍS (DOLORES) (1776)

This mission (415-621-8203) is located on Dolores Street, near 16th Street, in San Francisco. Tours are arranged by Greyline and the Mission is open from 9:00 A.M. to 5:00 P.M. daily.

It was June 29, 1776, when a small band of Spanish soldiers and settlers, with the three babies that had been born on the long march up from Mother Mexico, set up their fifteen tents on the banks of Laguna de los Dolores.

Then, one rainy Sunday in October of the same year, Father Serra welcomed, at Monterey, Captain Juan Bautista de Anza and his party of some two hundred pioneers. The travelers had come from Mexico to found a new colony, a fort, and a mission for Spain. The padres traveled northward with these new Californians and, within a few days' time, from a high hill they looked down on the bluest and largest bay they had ever seen. Here, they decided, would be a great place for an army force, if needed, and for trading ships from all over the world.

Redwood, a material foreign to those from Spain and Mexico, was hewn into rafters and sculptured into figures of patron saints. The church was built and the Indians were given some of the rights of apprenticeship. In their free time, they were allowed to work in the gardens raising onions, garlic, watermelon, and pumpkins.

The climate however was cold, with a penetrating fog that seeped over the lowlands far too often. Many of the mission Indians became ill and were sent to the Mission San Rafael; but,

111

for those who remained, some of the native customs were still encouraged, such as the tribal dances after the services.

Romanticists have long savored the tale of Maria Arguello, who waited with her brother one morning in 1806, at the San Francisco Presidio, for the arrival of the Imperial Chamberlain of Russia, Nikolai Petrovich Rezanov. The young, handsome emissary was coming to the Mission Dolores on an errand of mercy in behalf of his starving countrymen. Maria, dark-eyed and beautiful, and her brother José, were taking the place of their father, the Commandante. Rezanov, head of a great fur company and former Ambassador Extraordinary to Japan, had come from Sitka, Alaska, with a shipload of goods to barter for food.

Maria and Rezanov fell in love and pledged their love before the altar at the mission. He promised to return and bring Maria to the splendor of the Russian courts. But Rezanov never came back. Maria waited thirty years for her lover and then heard that he had died of fever on his return trip. Maria renounced her name and the world. She began a life which made her loved for years at the Mission San Francisco de Asís. As Sister Maria Dominica, she became California's first nun.

This romantic tale aside, San Francisco was a "Gold Town" and, during the exciting years of the boom, white tents could be seen all around the mission. Saturday night dances were given on the grounds following afternoons of the rowdy bear and bull fights.

Photos and paintings of the Mission Dolores give us a study of the remarkable—and sometimes sad—changes in its appearance. One, done in 1849, shows the "stars and stripes" much in evidence, the men on horseback supervising workers, the old Indian *carreta* still drawn by oxen, and a regular maze of weaving fence posts and fencing.

The well-remembered San Francisco earthquake of 1906

112

caused only minor ruptures in the Dolores Church, and the holocaust of the fire stopped just short of the mission.

More history can be found in the mission's cemetery than in the history books. Perhaps in no other mission churchyard do the tombstones give such a graphic picture of *presidio* life as in that of the Mission Dolores. Life was brief in those days—few headstones record lives of more than thirty-five years. The peril might be childbirth, a trip across the Bay, or perhaps a brawl in a saloon. These tombstones spell out many a tragedy and sorrow, like that of John and Anna Hart, who erected a monument to their six children, "flowers nipped as they began to bloom"; and of Athalie Baudichome, a young French bride who died with her two small children in the explosion of the steamboat *Jenny Lind*.

In 1952, Pope Pius XII bestowed upon the Mission Dolores the title of Minor Basilica. The parish church of San Francisco de Asis then became the first basilica west of the Mississippi, and the fourth in the United States. Mission Dolores qualified by fulfilling three requirements: it is a church that has been consecrated; it is one steeped in history which serves as an historical landmark and gives every appearance of permanence; and it is a place of pilgrimage.

Today, even though a huge highrise is being built almost within arm's length of the Mission Dolores, the fathers there have performed a remarkable feat by keeping the church looking almost as it did in 1791. The original bells are hung by rawhide in the bell tower, the garden is small but well-kept. Its treasures include the original bells from Mexico, the early confessional doors, a revolving tabernacle from Manila, and hand-carved altars and statues shipped from Mexico in 1780.

The mood is indeed one of quiet, reminiscent of life two centuries ago.

Mission San Rafael Arcángel.

20 MISSION SAN RAFAEL ARCÁNGEL (1817)

Mission San Rafael (415-456-3016) is located in San Rafael on Fifth Avenue and A Street, off Highway 101. It is open from 6:30 A.M. to 6:00 P.M. daily.

Bringing with them a hand-picked group of neophyte Indians from the Mission Dolores, four Franciscan Fathers dedicated the twentieth mission, San Rafael Arcángel, on December 14, 1817. Looking on were the native Indians of the area, the Coastal Miwok.

The Indians here ordinarily lived on salmon and lampreys and, for the most part, were quite peaceful. Yet, when one was killed in battle, the others would tear his limbs to pieces, place the top of his skull on a pike, and march with it triumphantly around the village.

The mortality rate at the Mission Dolores had been unusually high. The mission Indians suffered the debilitating effects of diseases that ran rampant while only one practicing physician had the impossible task of covering an entire California seacoast filled with patients. Sadly, the Franciscan Fathers had not been so well-schooled in medicine as in the arts, although a basic knowledge of simple surgery and medicine was part of the missionaries' curriculum. The Mission Dolores, hugging the foggy, damp seacoast, also had another problem—the harshness of the weather.

Father Luis Gil y Taboada volunteered for the new post at San Rafael. He was a Mexican-born priest who had two distinctive qualities which seemed to be especially needed at the hospital mission: one was that he was reported to be a skilled physician (indeed, he had performed both a Caesarean operation and delivered twins at the Mission Dolores), the other was his proficiency at Indian dialects.

Father Gil was satisfied that the move to a more favorable climate was justified, for he wrote that, of 209 baptisms, surely two-thirds would have died if left at the Dolores Mission. Twice Father Gil requested a transfer to his homeland of Mexico, for he suffered from *angina pectoris*. Twice his petition was granted, each time he threw away the desired papers, realizing that he was still very much needed by his neophytes.

When Father Gil died in 1833, his replacement was Father Juan Amoras who, according to the historian Hubert Howe Bancroft:

> ". . . was possessed of more than common ability, having great zeal, in every task successful. He was a successful business manager, a mechanic of more than ordinary skill and a kind missionary."

Father Amoras was further to prove his scientific skill by inventing a water clock which kept time for many years after his death.

Amoras was practical as well, and sent many parchments to his superiors asking for flocks of sheep so that the Indians could spin the wool and clothe themselves properly.

In 1824, the visiting Russian navigator, scientist, and trader, Otto von Kotzebue, admired the beautiful pasture land of San Rafael and its small deer. He commented on the diligence of the sentinels, who periodically rang a bell which was "answered every time by the bark of small foxlike wolves, which prowl about the mission."

Construction foremen today might be amazed at the detailed

reports the padres kept at the mission and sent to the Presidente concerning their neophyte work forces. Bricks were counted to the last one and surveys were kept on the production level of each Indian and each working group. The women and children were also scheduled and tallied as they carried the smaller stones. Although there certainly were no labor unions at that time, we have copies of such reports as:

> "Those who work at this task (making adobes) never work after eleven, never work on Saturday, and oftentimes do not work on Friday, because they complete their assigned tasks during the early part of the week. . . ."

In 1861, the ruins of the mission were purchased by a James Byers, for the use of the solid wood timbers at a time when lumber was costly.

San Rafael's active life was brief. Located in the H. M. DeYoung Museum in San Francisco are twenty-one oil paintings of the California missions. The artist represented each mission, not in the state of disrepair or decay of her time, but rather in their prime, drawing upon the memories of the early pioneers and of old sketches. In her rendition of the Mission San Rafael, however, starkness and simplicity almost overwhelm the viewer. The show of activity evident in most of the other paintings is lacking here. Two riders on horseback stand in the center of the picture but it is almost as if they had come upon a "ghost" mission.

With the financial assistance of the city of San Rafael and the Hearst Foundation, and at the insistence of the Marin County Historical Society, the mission was rebuilt as a nineteenth-century replica, with the original set of bells hanging in a rack in front of the mission. This restored mission has been designated as an official landmark of California.

117

Mission San Francisco Solano.

21 MISSION SAN FRANCISCO SOLANO (SONOMA MISSION) (1823)

Mission San Francisco Solano (415-938-4779) is located in Sonoma State Historic Park in Sonoma on State Highway 12. This State Historical Monument is open daily from 10:00 A.M. to 5:00 P.M., except Thanksgiving, Christmas, and New Year's Day.

The last, and most northerly, of the chain of twenty-one missions was the Mission San Francisco Solano, founded on July 4, 1823, by Padre José Altimira. Friar Altimira was young, brash, impatient with set rules, and, perhaps, a bit puffed-up as the close friend of the young commandante at the Presidio San Francisco, Captain Louis Arguello, who was later to become Governor. With no official approval, the padre began the construction of the buildings and corrals at Sonoma. There was a red-hot interchange of communiques until it was finally granted that Father Altimira could have his mission, and that the concept of combining the Missions San Rafael and Dolores with Solano would be dropped.

The early whitewashed and wooden-stucco chapel was erected, along with the priests' house, and a tower was made from the trunks of four trees. By 1827, the adobe chapel was rather grandiose for the locale, for it was two stories high and measured 152 by 33 feet. Then in 1838, the large chapel collapsed while being renovated during a series of sudden, heavy storms.

The teaching and discipline of the Indians, however, went steadily on. "Lies and juvenile delinquency were nearly unknown

119

among these people (the Indians) . . . ," Vinson Brown, a writer of the Sonoma Indians, tells us:

> "Ash devils (men covered with ashes) were used to handle, rather roughly, teenagers who had shown re-belliousness against group patterns of conduct. Usually afterward they became quite meek!"

Interest in this mission was not consistent. By 1846, Robert D. Parmelee, in his book, *Pioneer Sonoma,* reports that few of the North American pioneers cared what happened to the mission and that:

> "youthful Eliza Donner, survivor of the Donner tragedy, was fascinated with the mission belfry built of tree trunks in front of the priest's house and was continually tempted to ring the mission bells which hung by rawhide straps, from the smoothcut cross beams."

Parmelee also notes the variety of purposes that the mission was used for—a restaurant, an Indian employment agency, a home for a man and wife and five children, a blacksmith shop, and a magazine and newspaper shop.

Many people are amused at an early photograph, now in the California State Library, of the mission buildings, taken a short while after they were sold to Solomon Schocken. The Sonoma Valley Railroad passed within a few feet of the mission, a handy but, no doubt, very noisy bit of transportation for the padres to combat at their very doorstep. Reports have it that both the fathers and the parishioners found the railroad a constant source of annoyance. Evidently access had to give way to a more cloistered atmosphere and, by 1896, the railroad tracks had been removed.

120

Religious statuary abounds at the missions.

Even the priests' quarters had original uses. By the end of the nineteenth century, they were known as the Old Sonoma Winery. Further degradation came in 1907 when the mission buildings were used as a cow shed. A rather ribald saloon was only one-arm's length from the chapel itself.

But, by now, the message of the photographer was coming into its own, and Joseph Knowland brought many pictures of the sadly neglected mission buildings back to the California Historic Landmark League. The Native Sons and Daughters of the Golden West responded, in true patriotic fashion, in favor of the restoration of the mission.

By 1905, the saloon had been removed. But nostalgia had not quite become so "in" as it is today, and it wasn't until some fifteen years later that the old dilapidated hay wagon, and a cactus bush that was taller than a one-story house, disappeared. Also in 1905, a "good year" for the mission, the women of the Sonoma Valley raised funds for a new tin roof on part of the priests' quarters.

The mission collapsed, unfortunately, in 1909, and though the period of rebuilding soon began, the much-criticized cupola was gone and in its place was a plain cross. In 1914, the railroad tracks were relocated to the rear of the mission, and the trains carried excursions of picnickers and joyriders to Sonoma.

Today there is much to attract the visitor. The very colorful paintings on the ceilings, walls, and woodwork done by Richard Douglas, are evident in the interior of the church; and every year at least one tableau of mission days creates entertainment in an educational context for the townspeople and visitors to Sonoma.

Statue of padre.

BIBLIOGRAPHY

Armor, Samuel. *History of Orange County, California with Biographical Sketches.* Los Angeles: Historic Record Co., 1921.

Bancroft, Hubert Howe. *History of California,* Volumes 1-7. New York: McGraw-Hill, 1967.

Bauer, Helen. *California Mission Days.* New York: Doubleday & Co., Inc., 1951.

Bedford Jones, H. *The Mission and the Man.* Pasadena: San Pasqual Press, 1939.

Bell, Horace. *Reminiscences of a Ranger.* William Hebbird, 1927.

Bolton, Herbert Eugene. *Anza's California Expeditions.* New York: Russell & Russell, Vols. 1-6, 1966.

The California Missions. Menlo Park, California: Lane Book, Co., 1964.

Carrillo, Leo and Ainsworth. *The California I Love.* New Jersey: Prentice Hall, 1961.

Chapman, Charles E. *A History of California—the Spanish Period.* New York: The MacMillan Co., 1949.

Clinch, Bryan J. *California and Its Missions,* Vol. II. San Francisco: The Whitaker & Ray Company, 1904.

Corle, Edwin. *The Royal Highway.* Indianapolis: The Bobbs-Merrill Co., Inc., 1949.

Czarnowski, Lucile K. *Dances of Early California Days.* Palo Alto, California: Pacific Books, 1950.

de la Perouse. *A Voyage Round the World in the Years 1785, 1786, and 1788.* Published Conformably to the Decree of the National Assembly. Edited by M. L. A. Milet-Mureau, n.d.

Engelbert, Omer. *The Last of the Conquistador—Junípero Serra.* New York: Harcourt, Brace and Company, 1954.

Englehardt, Fr. Zephyrin. *San Juan Capistrano Mission.* Los Angeles: Standard Printing Co., 1922.

Geiger, Maynard (O.F.M., Ph.D.). *The History of California's Mission Santa Barbara.* Santa Barbara, California: Franciscan Fathers, n.d.

Gordon, Dudley. *Junípero Serra, California's First Citizen.* Los Angeles: Cultural Assets Press, 1969.

124

Hannau, Hans W. *The California Missions*. Garden City: Doubleday & Co., Inc., n.d.

Hawthorne, Hildegarde. *California's Missions*. New York: D. Appleton-Century Co., Inc., 1942.

The Indians of Mission Santa Barbara in Paganism and Christianity. Santa Barbara, California: Franciscan Fathers, 1960.

Jackson, Helen Hunt. *Glimpses of California and the Missions*. Little, Brown & Co., 1902.

James, George Wharton. *In and Out of the Old Missions of California*. Boston: Little, Brown & Co., 1918.

King, Kenneth M. *Mission to Paradise*. London: Burns & Oates, 1956.

Kroeber, Alfred L. *A Handbook of the Indians of California*. U.S. Government Bulletin 78, U.S. Series 1925.

La Purísima Mission. State of California. The Resources Agency, n.d.

McGroarty, John Steven. *California of the South, a History*. Chicago: S. J. Clarke Pub., 1933.

Mission San Juan Capistrano. Chicago: Curt Teich & Co., n.d.

Newcomb, Rexford. *The Old Mission Churches and Historic Houses of California*. Philadelphia: J. P. Lippincott Co., 1925.

Ogden, Adele. *California Sea Otter Trade 1784-1848*. Berkeley, California: University of California Press, 1941.

Orange County Newsmagazine. Volume 9, No. 2, February 1965.

Pleasants, Mrs. J. E. *History of Orange County*. Phoenix: J. R. Finnell & Co., n.d.

Rensch, Hero Eugene and Rensch, Ethel Grace. *California Missions*. Palo Alto: Stanford University Press, 1932.

Repplier, Agnes. *Junípero Serra*. New York: Doubleday Doran Co., 1933.

Riesenberg, Felix, Jr. *The Golden Road*. New York: McGraw-Hill Book Co., Inc., 1962.

—————. *The Story of California's Spanish Mission Trail*. New York: McGraw-Hill, 1962.

Roberts, Helen M. *Mission Tales,* Vol. 1. Palo Alto, California: Pacific Books, 1948.

Robinson, Alfred. *Life in California*. New York: Wiley & Putnam, 1846.

125

Saunders, Charles Francis and O'Sullivan, Father St. John. *Capistrano and Their Missions*. Boston: Houghton Mifflin Co., 1915.

Saunders, Charles Francis and Father St. John O'Sullivan. *Capistrano Nights*. New York: Robert M. McBride & Co., 1930.

Stern, Alec. *Etchings of California Missions*. San Mateo, n.d.

Stevenson, T. E. *Caminos Viejos*. Special publication of Santa Ana Junior College, 1930.

W.P.A. *Workers of The Writer's Programs, Los Angeles*. New York: Hastings House, 1951.

Walsh, Marie T. *The Mission Bells of California*. San Francisco: Harr Wagner Pub. Co., 1934.

Webb, Edith Buckland. *Indian Life at the Old Missions*. Los Angeles: Warren F. Lewis, 1952.

Wright, Ralph B.; Anderson, John B.; and Watson, Benjamin M., editors. *The California Mission*. Los Angeles: The Sterling Press, 1950.

Your California. California Bicentennial Series, Standard Oil Company of California, n.d.

$2.95 EACH—WESTERN TRAVEL & LEISURE GUIDEBOOKS FROM THE WARD RITCHIE PRESS

Trips for the Day, Weekend or Longer

MOST BOOKS HAVE PHOTOGRAPHS AND MAPS.

QUANTITY		TOTAL
☐	**BACKYARD TREASURE HUNTING**	$ _____
☐	**BAJA CALIFORNIA:** Vanished Missions, Lost Treasures, Strange Stories True and Tall	$ _____
☐	**BICYCLE TOURING IN LOS ANGELES**	$ _____
☐	**EAT,** A Toothsome Tour of L.A.'s Specialty Restaurants	$ _____
☐	**EXPLORING BIG SUR, MONTEREY AND CARMEL**	$ _____
☐	**EXPLORING CALIFORNIA BYWAYS, No. 2,** In and Around Los Angeles	$ _____
☐	**EXPLORING CALIFORNIA BYWAYS, No. 3,** Desert Country	$ _____
☐	**EXPLORING CALIFORNIA BYWAYS, No. 4,** Mountain Country	$ _____
☐	**EXPLORING CALIFORNIA BYWAYS, No. 5,** Historic Sites of California	$ _____
☐	**EXPLORING CALIFORNIA BYWAYS, No. 6,** Owens Valley	$ _____
☐	**EXPLORING CALIFORNIA BYWAYS, No. 7,** An Historical Sketchbook	$ _____
☐	**EXPLORING CALIFORNIA FOLKLORE**	$ _____
☐	**EXPLORING THE GHOST TOWN DESERT**	$ _____
☐	**EXPLORING HISTORIC CALIFORNIA**	$ _____
☐	**EXPLORING THE MOTHER LODE COUNTRY**	$ _____
☐	**EXPLORING SMALL TOWNS, No. 1**—Southern California	$ _____
☐	**EXPLORING SMALL TOWNS, No. 2**—Northern California	$ _____
☐	**EXPLORING THE UNSPOILED WEST, Vol. 1**	$ _____
☐	**EXPLORING THE UNSPOILED WEST, Vol. 2**	$ _____
☐	**FEET FIRST:** Walks through Ten Los Angeles Areas	$ _____
☐	**GREAT BIKE TOURS IN NORTHERN CALIFORNIA**	$ _____
☐	**GUIDEBOOK TO THE CANYONLANDS COUNTRY**	$ _____
☐	**GUIDEBOOK TO THE COLORADO DESERT OF CALIFORNIA**	$ _____
☐	**GUIDEBOOK TO THE FEATHER RIVER COUNTRY**	$ _____
☐	**GUIDEBOOK TO THE LAKE TAHOE COUNTRY, Vol. I.** Echo Summit, Squaw Valley and the California Shore	$ _____
☐	**GUIDEBOOK TO THE LAKE TAHOE COUNTRY, Vol. II.** Alpine County, Donner-Truckee, and the Nevada Shore	$ _____

[MORE BOOKS AND ORDER FORM ON OTHER SIDE]

- ☐ **GUIDEBOOK TO LAS VEGAS** $ _____
- ☐ **GUIDEBOOK TO LOST WESTERN TREASURE** $ _____
- ☐ **GUIDEBOOK TO THE MISSIONS OF CALIFORNIA** $ _____
- ☐ **GUIDEBOOK TO THE MOUNTAINS OF SAN DIEGO AND ORANGE COUNTIES** $ _____
- ☐ **GUIDEBOOK TO THE NORTHERN CALIFORNIA COAST, VOL. I.** Highway 1 $ _____
- ☐ **GUIDEBOOK TO PUGET SOUND** $ _____
- ☐ **GUIDEBOOK TO RURAL CALIFORNIA** $ _____
- ☐ **GUIDEBOOK TO THE SACRAMENTO DELTA COUNTRY** $ _____
- ☐ **GUIDEBOOK TO THE SAN BERNARDINO MOUNTAINS OF CALIFORNIA,** Including Lake Arrowhead and Big Bear $ _____
- ☐ **GUIDEBOOK TO THE SAN GABRIEL MOUNTAINS OF CALIFORNIA** $ _____
- ☐ **GUIDEBOOK TO SALTWATER FISHING IN SOUTHERN CALIFORNIA** $ _____
- ☐ **GUIDEBOOK TO THE SPAS OF NORTHERN CALIFORNIA** $ _____
- ☐ **GUIDEBOOK TO VANCOUVER ISLAND** $ _____
- ☐ **HIKING THE SANTA BARBARA BACKCOUNTRY** $ _____
- ☐ **SABRETOOTH CATS AND IMPERIAL MAMMOTHS** $ _____
- ☐ **SKI LOS ANGELES** $ _____
- ☐ **WHERE TO TAKE YOUR CHILDREN IN NEVADA** $ _____
- ☐ **WHERE TO TAKE YOUR CHILDREN IN NORTHERN CALIFORNIA** $ _____
- ☐ **WHERE TO TAKE YOUR CHILDREN IN SOUTHERN CALIFORNIA** $ _____
- ☐ **WHERE TO TAKE YOUR GUESTS IN SOUTHERN CALIFORNIA** $ _____
- ☐ **YOUR LEISURE TIME . . . HOW TO ENJOY IT** $ _____

THE WARD RITCHIE PRESS
474 S. Arroyo Parkway, Pasadena, Calif. 91105

Please send me the Western Travel and Leisure Guidebooks I have checked. I am enclosing $_____ (check or money order). Please include 25¢ per copy to cover mailing costs. California residents add state sales tax.

Name _____

Address _____

City _____ State _____ Zip Code _____